The Rise of an Orphan Generation

Longing for a Father

By Harry Salem II

Scripture within text appears in italics.

The Rise of an Orphan Generation: Longing for a Father

ISBN 1-890370-24-X

Printed in Canada

PO Box 701287

Tulsa, OK 74170

www.salemfamilyministries.org

The Rise of an Orphan Generation: Longing for a Father

Dedication

By Harry Salem II

I dedicate this book to our two sons who remain on the earth with us. Having two children awaiting us in heaven, makes the time we have with our two sons here on earth even more precious and valuable. Since this is a collaboration of Salem men, we dedicate this book to each other.

To our first born Harry III, thank you for your strength, your bluntness, your unfailing love and your matter-of-factness that sometimes makes me want to pull out what hair I have left, but always is a breath of fresh air. You have taught me to always be true to myself, to be who God has made me to be, to never be intimidated to tell the truth, even if it is not what others want to hear. Thank you.

To our second born, Roman, thank you for your joy, overflowing life and love you continually bring in our home. Your huge smile and multitude of words can overwhelm me at times to the point I don't even know how to respond to you! You have shown me how to have fun, to love and to live each day to the fullest. You hurt the old guy in basketball but even the pain is fun coming from you!

To our wonderful and amazing sons, Harry III, and Roman, I dedicate this book to you. Thank you for teaching me how to be a father. Thank you for your patience with me as I struggled to learn from our Father God how to be what each of you needed me to be in your lives.

To our son, Malachi, who we lost in a miscarriage; I have never met you, but I know you by the Spirit of God. I know you are an amazing young man and we will make up for lost earth years on the other side of eternity.

To our one and only 'queen bee' daughter, Gabrielle; you are one of a kind! There is no one like you, my girl. Your six years of life on this earth were more filled with love and life than most people live in 100 years! You taught me how to long for my heavenly Father because I miss you so very much. We will do all the father/daughter things once I arrive in your glorious place of residence. I won't come too soon, but until we are together again, my heart longs for you... just a little less than I long for Jesus and my eternal Father. Thank you for teaching me how important being a father really is. Keep the door open in our mansion in the sky - I'll know it because it will be the pink one that looks like your fold-out Barbie house you had here.

To our children, for whom I strove to be a better father, but as I found out, it's better to be a papa than a father because children instinctively love their fathers but children choose to love their papas.

I love you all,

Papa

Harry III, Mama, Gabrielle,

Dad & Roman

1998

Foreword

By Harry Salem III

(Our Lil' Harry)

In this day and age, growing up isn't easy. Many children around the world have so many different problems because of who they have as parents. Children can sometimes have parents who ignore them and their daily needs, parents who don't really care about them or what they do in life, parents who get divorced and neglect their kids, parents who abandon or abuse them, etc. A lot of kids are in a real mess because people just don't get that it takes a real effort to be a father or mother. It takes all the time and patience in the world to properly raise a kid and to see what they need in life. In truth, it takes a really different kind of person to be a parent. Someone who is responsible, careful with things, who looks toward the future, puts others before themselves, listens, provides for others, participates with others, works hard, has patience, and who tries to keep everything on the right track in life. To a small degree, these are at least the basic qualities that a person should have if they are to be a good parent.

In my life, I have seen many people that have been good parents. I have met and known people that have taken the responsibility to raise their kids right and be in their lives. I have also seen the kind of people that are ultimately unfit to be parents. I am in college now, I have a job, and I have a chance at a good life. I want to say that I was blessed with the chance to be able to do all of this by God, but that would only be half of the truth. God did give me the chance at a good life, but more to the point, it was the people that He put into my life that ultimately showed me how to get to that good life. I was given two good parents that put me before themselves. I have parents who took part in my life, saw what needed to be put into my life and what needed to be taken out or avoided. I have parents who gave me a good education and taught me important life lessons that they knew I should learn. I have parents who didn't force God on me but instead let me get to know Him, and establish my own relationship with Him. My parents were also people that would take time to participate in my life and let me know that they were there for me whenever I needed them.

They say that people in life often try to find a hero for themselves, or someone they aspire to be like. Some idolize sports figures like baseball and basketball players. A lot of people choose politicians who become senators, congressmen, or even presidents as their heroes. People can even like fictional characters like superheroes or action heroes that fight evil or save the day for the average person as someone they can look up to. In my life, I have seen great athletes and politicians. I've read all the comic books about big-time superheroes fighting all the evil villains and saving the day. It's all pretty cool stuff, and wanting to do things like this in life is a really good idea for a goal in the future. The thing is I don't know any of these people. I don't know what their lives are filled with, or what they do when they're not on public display. And all the fictional heroes that I read about are just that, fictional characters. Comic book heroes aren't even real, so why should I make them my own personal hero? I have had only one real hero in my entire life. I have really only known one man that has been really honest and truthful with me on all things, taught me important things, played with me, loved me unconditionally through everything, and stayed and participated in my life when I needed it the most. That person is my father, and he is a one of a kind hero to me.

I remember when my dad used to come home every day after work. I would be done with school, and I would sit in our kitchen playing with my toys or drawing in my books (more like scribbling, but I did stay in the lines). I would just wait there until he got home. Whenever I heard the garage door open, I would jump to my feet and stand next to the refrigerator ready to give him a hug. When he would come through the door, I would run up to him, hug him, and see a smile on his face that always made me happy. To some, he appeared as an average working man coming home after a 9 to 5 day wearing a suit and carrying a briefcase. To me though, he was the best thing that I would see all day.

On Saturdays, after a long week at doing the things that kids do, like school, baseball, homework, and chores, it was time for leisure time. I would watch my cartoons in the morning till eleven, and then in would come my dad. It was a pretty fun time. I would play with my toys, and he and I would watch Bob Vila build houses just before the local golf tournaments would come on. It might seem like construction and golf shows would be boring to a kid, but as long as I got to spend time with my dad, that made it fun enough. I would have a lot of fun doing little things like this with him, but I would be in the greatest of spirits when I did the really big things with my father.

When I was younger, I played baseball and basketball like a lot of kids did. I wasn't great, but I was able to win a couple of trophies here and there if I played hard enough. No matter when my games were, or where they were, my father always did his best to come to them. I remember this one particular night during a championship baseball game. It was on a night that dad had to usually work late and I thought he might not show up. I understood (at that time) that he had his work, and once in awhile a person just can't get away from it because it's important. Anyway, as the game was basically still beginning and I'm out in the outfield waiting for the first batter to hit, I look over my shoulder because I hear a car pulling up. I couldn't believe my eyes! Coming out of the car in his nice work suit and into a muddy little league field is none other than my father. That was not only a surprise, but something that made that night a real special event for me. My team not only won the game, but I was given the chance to have my father watching me at the same time. It seems like my father always knows when to be there at the right time for me.

In my life, my father has always been a great influence on my life. He has given me the chance to do what I wanted to do in life by constantly encouraging me to always see everything I do through to the end. I have accomplished so much of what I desired to do in my life because of his influence and guidance. Whenever things in my life got hard or difficult and I really needed a friend to just help me out with things, I could always come to my father and he would be willing to help me out with whatever I needed. No matter what the problem, I could always count on him for anything.

I remember when I left for college out of state. I was ready to go and everyone was wishing me well as I started a new chapter in my life. That morning, my father was very emotional, and when it came time to leave, he went over to the side of my truck and did something that I only saw him do two other times in my life. He went to the side of my truck and began to cry. My father was sad that I was leaving. He was going to miss me. It was as though he knew that once I left my drive way, things would forever be different. As I saw the tears in his eyes, I knew right then and there just how much my father deeply loved me as his son. I just walked over and began to cry with him. I told him that I wouldn't be leaving him, but that I was beginning a new step, a new level in my life that he would be a part of. That was all I could say, but it still wasn't enough to keep him from crying. I left him that day, but I called him every day, and I always made sure to tell him that I loved him no matter where I was or what I was doing. I still remember that moment every day of my life. The day my father cried because he loves me.

Life is extremely hard, and there are not many people that will always give up their lives for you. I am very blessed to have such a person in my life, especially in the form of my father. From him, I have learned to do my very best to put others before myself. From him, I learned to love people deeper than I ever could. I was given a chance to lead a life that is very rare because of him. The kind of life he has given me is one of significance and a deep conscious choice to live life to the fullest. The last thing that I will say is this. I love my father with all my heart. I thank God every day for him, and that my relationship with him is better than anything that I could ever ask for. My father, the man I call my hero.

I love you, Dad.

H3

Harry III, getting his college degree.

My son said to me, “I did this for you,” and handed me his diploma.

I asked him, “Why son?” He answered, “Because you don’t have one, Dad.”

Foreword

By Roman Salem

Fathers and dads. These are two words that have the same meaning to most people, but if you know the difference, they can be worlds apart. A dad buys you toys, helps you with your homework, tells you about girls, plays with you, teaches you about cars, buys you a car, is your friend, gives you a hug after you hit the game winning shot, and on and on the wonderful definitions of dad. But a father gives you his time, guides you down the right path, teaches you respect for yourself and for others, teaches you how to drive, protects you when no one else can, and when you miss the shot to win and feel the world on your shoulders, a father is there to put part of the weight on his shoulders and lets you know you are always loved.

I was born and like most kids had a dad but I was blessed by God and He gave me a father. Growing up I never really understood the difference of a father and a dad, but along the road of life I have learned about the two. I had friends who had families like mine and I had some that didn't have the blessing I did. I remember talking to my friend about how much fun I had with my father the day before and he said, "I only see my dad before work while he stands in front of the mirror shaving."

I began to imagine that at seven years old what if I only saw my father shaving. My father worked from 9:00 a.m. to 7:00 p.m. (if he was lucky enough to get off that early). I remember him coming home tired from a long day of work, exhausted really. He would see me sitting with my basketball at the back door in anticipation to see his car coming around the corner just to give him a hug. It would have been perfectly normal to change from a suit to his pajamas and relax for the few remaining hours of the night. But not my father. He would run up the stairs to not waste any daylight, and toss on his basketball clothes, pick me up, and carry me outside to play a little one on one. I was seven years old then. Now fourteen years later, the roles have reversed somewhat. I have a job now on top of school, but I never miss some one on one time with my dad, and if possible we try to make that time be every day.

I remember weekends at home with my family, my brother watching cartoons, mom in the kitchen making breakfast, and where is my dad? He has been outside working on the yard since sunrise already having a long week of work; but also, getting up at the crack of dawn to do the chores. My mom asked me to go get him for breakfast and I did as my mother asked. I told my dad the food was ready and on the table. We started to walk back to the house when I had to ask him, "Dad, why do you do all this for yourself? Why does it matter?"

I received an answer I didn't expect. He said, "Son, I don't do this just for me. I do this for you guys as well."

I asked, "How so?" He said, "I mow the lawn, trim the hedges, and plant flowers because your mom likes to have a beautiful yard. I clean the pool so you kids can have a nice place to swim. I fix your bike so you can ride today."

I had another question, "Dad, what part of all of that was for you?" He simply answered, "Because it brings me joy to watch my family be so happy and enjoy these outdoor activities."

To this day my dad will get up early to not wash his own car, but to wash his sons' cars, mine and Harry's. He does it not because they are covered in dirt or we ask him to do it. But because he says and I quote, "You boys deserve a clean car to drive around in." That's our dad. Now it's a race for us to be up before him if possible and instead of him washing our cars, we try and beat him to it and wash his first, and then ours!

Throughout high school I played sports but my passion was and still is basketball. My dad was at every game I played in high school, even when I didn't think it was possible for him to be there. I remember one weekend in particular that he had flown out to preach and we were having an away game. His flight was set to come in two hours ahead of my game with plenty of time to drive out and see me. It was in the middle of the day and his flight had been delayed, and then cancelled due to weather. Once again, my dad turned into a super hero, changing flights, changing airlines, landing in another city, renting a car, and bounding into the gym three seconds before tip-off!

While I was in school my dad was my 'get out of homework' free card. I could use it to my advantage with my mother. I would go help my dad with anything I could to skip homework. I think he knew that deep down my motives were not the best ones! And I believe that's why he took it upon himself to teach me knowledge, maybe not from a book or a formula, but he taught me good morals, strong belief in Jesus, and wisdom. You see, although I grew up in church, my dad led me through the sinners' prayer and helped me dedicate my life to God.

I will always remember the day my mom left on a video of a minister about the end times, the rapture, and people being left behind who had been good people, and had been in church all their lives. I was so afraid of how and what I saw on that video and it made me take a look at what I was doing in my own life. I knew I had to get right with the Lord.

I looked through the house trying to find Mom, but I couldn't find her. Dad was on the couch taking a nap. For me it was one of the hardest things in the world to do, to ask my Dad to help me make sure I was going to heaven. I knew it had to be done, and it had to be done right then! I mustered up the courage and asked him to help me. It was truly a great moment for me as my earthly father led me to my heavenly Father.

My dad has always been a role model for me; he's always been hard working, honest, loving, and a caring man. I have been blessed to have a man like him rear me and influence me and my life behaviors. My dad has taught me to put others first and lead by example, not just saying one thing and doing another. No matter what or when I might have gotten myself into a mess, he was and I know for sure he will always be there to give me a helping hand in any way possible.

My dad has given me every way possible to succeed, even if I take it for granted sometimes. My father worked so hard his whole life to give me a better one than he has had. He has done this to bless me with the things he never had growing up, especially since he didn't have his dad.

I know my grandfather passed away when my dad was ten years old. When I think about that I can't help but think about what my life would have been if that had been me. How different would my life have been if my dad had passed away when I was ten years old? I know one thing for sure; I would not have turned out to be a tenth of the man my father is. I do not know if I could have overcome that terrible adversity. It truly astounds me to think about how my father at ten years old was thrust into a situation of becoming a man and somehow with the grace of God, he ran with it.

My dad has become a great man not only in the eyes of the world but in the eyes of God. When we were younger we always looked at our fathers as supermen, but as we grow up we see them as Clark Kent. In my case, my dad never really stopped being my hero. Sure he can't fly or stop bullets, but he is a realistic, bona fide super hero. He is a man who puts his family first, a hard-working person with morals, standards, honor and integrity for himself and his children. He is a man who would do anything for his son even stand in front of a bullet if one was coming at me. He's a hero and we should all strive to become like him. As I have gotten older, I see those impossible things that I didn't think could have been accomplished and yet, he did them all with ease.

To me being a father means putting your family before yourself, taking a step back from your own life, and giving it all to your kids, not because you have to, but because you want to. It means to love your family no matter what happens, and to be a strong leader for the ones you care about. How did I come to understand my definition of father? Dad? Because that's the dad and father I have watched in my life for twenty-one years so far.

Thanks Dad, you did more for me than you will ever know.

I love you, Pop.

Your son,

Roman

Roman, graduating from High School.

Preface

By Harry Salem II

When Cheryl and I began our family, during those first nine months of pregnancy, we were determined to do it right. Cheryl got this teaching on supernatural childbirth and was determined to have exactly that! I can honestly say for me, supernatural painless childbirth is exactly what I got! Childbirth for me was painless. I thought it was super! Being a parent was absolutely natural for me! As my wife reminded me, "Yeah, all you did was sit by while I did all the work. And even when they asked you to stand up and cut the cord, you forgot how to work your legs! Super-natural-painless… I don't think so! And by the way, it is the Lamaze method, not the Le Mans car! You never did figure that out!" My way of being Cheryl's coach in childbirth was finding her a good friend who would coach her all the way through to the end. I kept saying, "I sure wish this baby would get here. Can't you go any faster?!" It's a real miracle that I actually survived childbirth!

Now that you know a little about our relationship as parents, I have asked my wife, the mother of our four children, to write the introduction of this book to you. She has been the driving force for me to have an intimate relationship with my heavenly Father and I know no one else who has such a great

Father/daughter relationship with the Lord than Cheryl. I can only pray that when I stand before my heavenly Father that He tells me that I took care of His earthly daughter, my wife, better than anyone else. As a husband, I want to hear Him say, "Well done, son."

Introduction

By Cheryl Salem

Over the years I have written many introductions to books, but none with more pleasure or gratitude in my heart than this one. I married Harry Salem decades ago. I was a traveling minister who had decided that there was not a man on the earth strong enough to be married to me with my 'strong as shoe leather' personality, and the deepest of callings by the Holy Spirit to preach the gospel of Jesus Christ. I was a guest on a Christian television show and I saw this very somber, tall, dark, and handsome man across the room. I was not looking, mind you, but he was hard to miss!

As my eyes landed on his character, and I do mean, his character, as Harry is the only person I have ever seen that can display his very nature in the way he simply stands! I saw him and immediately heard the voice of the Holy Spirit within me say, "There's a man strong enough to cover you."

Needless to say, if I had known at that moment what that really meant I would have run for the exit! What is best for us and what we usually want are very seldom the same things! I can't help but smile as I write these words, as the Lord has used Harry Salem more than any human on the earth to help me become the woman of God He intended for me to be. I regret nothing, not one minute. I never wanted to divorce him, even though I begged God more than once to 'smite him down'... or me! Just get one of us out of this misery! I'm laughing hard as I write this because it has been through this amazing man of God that I have learned so much about the nature of our Father God.

Harry has taught me that we don't need to 'see it' to 'be it.' We don't have to look for a trail already traveled, and go that way; he has taught me to cut a path where no one has ever gone, and give others an opportunity to follow.

This book can help you get over yourself, turn lose of your past, break free from the lies of the enemy and from those voices telling you that you will never know the love of a father, or be the true father that you long to be.

I have watched the progression of a man emotionally crippled by rejection and abandonment issues and spirits. I have watched his heart be broken, as he crawled to the Father God with the two broken pieces of his heart in his hands, to lay them at the Father's feet with no understanding, and yet unyielding faith-filled words crying out from his lips, "Lord, I trust You."

Whether you have had a normal father/son life and want to know a deeper relationship, or whether you are more like Harry, growing up without a father, and searching diligently through years of learning how to be what you did not have, this book is for you. Enjoy it, laugh with it, cry with it, and get mad in it, if you must, but learn from it. Let Harry's journey point the way to the Father your heart longs for already.

Get ready to be changed; get ready to be challenged.

Harry's favorite scripture has become Matthew 6:21, *"For where your treasure is, there your heart will be also."* (NKJV)

Through these pages you will see very clearly where Harry's heart is... by what he treasures. He has spent a lifetime in pursuit of a God-kind of relationship with his children. I have heard Harry say this so many times over the years. "I was born a male, but I choose to become a man... God's man."

Cheryl & Harry

Chapter One

My Desire to Have a Father

It was a typical fall day in November. Not quite Thanksgiving, in fact, just barely past the candy of Halloween. I was ten years old and the youngest child, the only male child, in an ethnic Lebanese family. I was born third in the rank and file of Salem children, which carries meaning in the Middle Eastern culture into which I was born. You see, my father, a onetime golden glove boxer in the United States Marine Corps, who was swarthy and handsome and first generation Lebanese American after his parents moved to Michigan from Lebanon, married a non-Lebanese woman. Harry Salem met Patricia Christensen, a stylish, petite, beautiful lady of Danish descent, and our little family began to take shape. First my sister was born. A girl, hmm... not to be confused with a male child! Oh, girls were fine, but in the Lebanese culture, it was the boys who carried on the family name - the line of succession came through the name. Of course, girls would always grow up and marry someone else, and thus, the name change! Time went by and my mom produced another baby, once again, a girl. Still no male for my father's family, no male heir!

Then came the amazingly victorious day on August 27, 1958 when all became right with the world. I was born! A male child was born, with all the right parts to make my Danish mother acceptable in the culture of my father. At least she could produce a male child! As glorious as I am quite certain the angels sang when I was born, it didn't seem to inspire my father to spend any more time at home. My dad was a workaholic like no other. My dad was the provider of all providers. My dad was larger than life. He was the president of the automobile dealers of Michigan in our great state. He owned the Lincoln/Mercury dealership in the great GM town of Flint, Michigan.

Harry II & Harry Sr. at the Dealership.

As I grew up being mothered by the best mother in the whole world, I was fathered by an absent dad. Don't get me wrong. He was not any different than most men of that generation. They were taught to work hard, provide much, love from a distance, and not feel any pressure to get involved in the rearing of the children. He fulfilled all of this marvelously.

When I needed a new baseball glove, he would call the man at the athletic store and arrange payment for whatever my mother and I picked out. My mother came to all the games. My mother drove us to and from... well, everywhere. Except to school, which my dad did on his way to work, and those were memorable journeys! How can everyday journeys to school be memorable? My father was notorious for just grabbing any car off the lot and driving it home and on a regular basis, those cars would run out of gas on our way to school. With my dad everything was a last minute journey. My mother was involved in our lives 100%. My dad? *He provided for us*. He provided food, clothes, shelter, and safety... all the necessities of life were ours because of my father.

My father was a marine and once a marine always a marine. And as much as he was a dedicated marine, he was that dedicated to his business and work. We didn't see him that much but when we did, if he told me to take out the trash, I took out the trash. If there was no trash in the basket, I crumpled up some paper and took it out! No questions, no explanations, no back-talking or discussion. He said it, I did it. It was always yes sir, no sir, and yes ma'am, no ma'am. Discipline and respect were first and foremost in our home.

When it was time for Christmas gifts to be purchased, my father would make arrangements with a store for my mother to be able to purchase what she needed. If she needed a man to help her pick out something, my father would make arrangements with his brother, my uncle, to go with my mom, or with me. My father took care of everything, except one thing. I did not have a dad.

Let's get back to my story. It was a typical fall day, November in Michigan. It was 1968, I was ten years old, and my father had been diagnosed with a very serious disease, and was given only a short time to live. He had leukemia. His condition deteriorated quickly. Within six months, he was gone.

My mother and grandfather came home from the hospital in the middle of the night, awakened me, and had me get every picture of my dad and put them all in the closet. She then had me sit down beside her on the couch and she put her head in my lap and went to sleep. From that day forth, I was the man of the house. (Many men in my life told me that statement over and over.) Please don't do this to a child! You will steal their childhood and they will never get to experience all of life.

It didn't start there, really. On my last trip to the hospital to see my dad, he had me stand beside his bed and he looked me square in the eyes and with these words he set my destiny in motion. "You are going to be the man of the house now. Don't trust anyone. Don't be a sucker for anyone. Don't cry at my funeral." So I had my marching orders from that day forward. I knew I had to be tough. As tough as a ten-year-old boy with a broken-hearted mother could be. I tried, I really did, to do everything my dad had told me to do. I spent the next few decades trying to live up to those fateful words, delivered to me by my father, on his death bed.

But my destiny was not that easily set by the words of my dying father. Oh, of course, for many years I did my best to fulfill the destiny set by my earthly father, but God has a plan and purpose for us that is far beyond the human words spoken over us. We can change the course of our destiny simply by longing for more than human purposes. We can long for a Father who knows no boundaries, who knows no limits, and who knows everything, everywhere. My eternal Father has a plan set for me that is for my good and not for evil. By longing for a true father, I began to long for a true destiny, one set from eternity and not by man.

No matter how many years it takes to break away from the wrong words spoken over you as a child, don't give up! Don't stop! Run as far as you can get from those destructive words. Run to the one who knows more, sees more, and IS more than all our pasts combined. Who is He? He is our future! He is our Father.

When you are first trying to break free from the past, it can feel like you are attached to a bungee cord. You can get further away only to be pulled back even deeper to those past feelings. That 'nature' that was put in you as a child is drawn upon by people in your life. It becomes part of your character and whether it is good or bad, it's a trait within you. But you can get free from it if you can identify it. My traits of rigid strength and stoicism were capitalized upon and used by other people. But it wasn't who I knew I was deep inside my heart.

Sometimes you have to take a step back to see how close you are to your destiny. Once you can identify and recognize your faults then you can change your future!

I recognized it and worked hard to change it. I also saw that I had been a product of my environment. Sometimes to change what your surroundings have made you to be, you have to change your surroundings to get a fighting chance. Now, I am not saying you need to quit your job or get a divorce!

If you can change the way you think, then you can change where you are going.

All I am saying is ask the Lord to help you recognize what has you captive, and take those thoughts captive. Your future freedom lies within your own mind. If you can change the way you think, then you can change where you are going.

In the Bible, in the book of I Samuel, there is a story about a young boy whose name, of course, was Samuel. His mother had begged God to give her a son, and had dedicated him to the Lord. Samuel was that son. From the time he was weaned, he was taken to the house of the Lord in Shiloh and lent to the Lord in the care of Eli the priest.

In chapter three we see that as Samuel grew, he ministered before the Lord, even as a child. Eli the priest had wicked sons but Samuel, who was lent to the Lord, stayed very faithful to the Lord and to Eli the priest. One night as Eli was lying down in his place, and while Samuel was also lying down for the evening, the Lord called Samuel. And Samuel answered, "Here I am!"

Picking up the story in I Samuel 3:5-11, *So he ran to Eli and said, "Here I am, for you called me." And he said, "I did not call; lie down again." And he went and lay down. Then the Lord called yet again, "Samuel!" So Samuel arose and went to Eli, and said, "Here I am, for you called me." Eli answered, "I did not call, my son; lie down again."*

(Now Samuel did not yet know the Lord, nor was the word of the Lord yet revealed to him.) And the Lord called Samuel again the third time. So he arose and went to Eli, and said, "Here I am, for you did call me." Then Eli perceived that the Lord had called the boy. Therefore Eli said to Samuel, "Go lie down; and it shall be, if He calls you, that you must say, 'Speak, Lord, for Your servant hears.'"

Then the Lord said to Samuel; "Behold, I will do something in Israel at which both ears of everyone who hears it will tingle."

God gave Samuel more instructions about what was about to happen to the house of Eli and his wicked sons. Samuel was talked to by God as a young boy repeatedly, but it was Eli the old man, who recognized that God was speaking and told Samuel how to respond to God. Samuel did not change his surroundings physically, but he changed his surroundings mentally.

Eli told him to stop listening for his priestly father's voice, but to listen to the voice of his heavenly Father. Once Samuel had proper instructions as to how to hear the voice of the Lord, he not only heard but he obeyed the voice.

Eli told Samuel to go back and lie down, to do exactly what he was doing before, but this time, listen for God to speak to him. Listen for God to talk to you. God wants to talk to you. All He needs you to do is recognize His voice and start listening!

Samuel didn't change his actual surroundings but he changed his environment by actively listening for the voice of the Lord. Once Samuel had proper instructions on what was actually happening as he heard the voice of the Lord, he replied, "Speak, for Your servant hears!"

What awesome words those must be to the Lord's ears when we actually acknowledge His voice and respond to Him that we are listening! Sometimes we think we hear people speak into our lives but it doesn't seem to stick. It's because we are only hearing them as humans, mere people. It's time to recognize these elders, like Eli, that God has placed in our lives who have been there for us and listen to what they are saying so we can actually learn these things which can take us from where we are to where we need to be. These are called "Fathering Moments!"

The Bible says there are many teachers but few fathers. (I Corinthians 4:15 AMP) Fathers take time to impart into the lives of chosen sons around them to help in their future and success. Teachers only teach to the student what success should be in their lives. You wouldn't want a teacher to teach failure! But fathers humble themselves to help you, impart to you, to help make you a better you! A great old book that I use to read every year is, [4]*How I Raised Myself from Failure to Success in Selling*, by Frank Bettger. It's a simple read, but a great, true story and its principles can be applied to any walk of life at any time in ones' life.

Chapter Two

Determined to be a Great Father

I heard this quote once, "A fatherless child thinks all things are possible, but nothing is safe."

I was determined when my time came to have children that I was going to be the perfect father. I was not going to abandon my children or squander the time that I was given with them. As work pressed in and pressures of life followed, the quality time I spent with them seemed to dwindle. This was not because I wanted it that way, but the circumstances of life were little by little stealing my time.

For every minute that I felt was lost between our children and me, I blamed circumstances, situations, life, and anybody else that got in my line of sight!

I began to realize that the most valuable thing in my life was my time. Time. When we are young, it seems to drag by, minute by minute. As adults it seems to fly by, year by year. Regardless of our age, or our perception of time, it is indeed the most valuable possession we have here on earth.

One of the greatest realizations of my time spent with my children was when I looked in the mirror and said, "The buck stops with me." When my time is taken from me, it is not stolen, for no one can steal it from me. I can only give it away, and the buck stops with me. I began to realize that I am responsible for how much time I give my children. I began to see that the use of my time was in my hands not in others. I saw that with much prayer and organization, planning and determination I could dictate by my desires where my time would be spent.

> I am responsible for how much time I give my children.

Matthew 6:21

"For where your treasure is, there your heart will be also."

When we are kids all we think about is being an adult. When we are adults all we think about is being a kid! That's why so many men today play video games, trying to relive their child-like times. That's why grandparents love to be with the grandkids! It rekindles their youth simply by association.

The things upon which I place the most value, there is where you will find my heart. If I value work, then my heart will always be at work. If I value golf, then my heart will always be on the golf course. If I value my wife, then my heart will always be with my wife. If I value my children, then my heart will always be with my children. If I value my God, then my heart will always be with my God.

Whatever we put value upon, our heart will always follow. Where our heart is, our time and effort will always follow. The value I place upon my children will be evident by the time I spend with them, as well as my heart towards them.

I had to change the way I perceived my life, my value, my treasures, and most of all the relationships around me. I had to realize that my children did not come from me, they came through me, and that I only have a short time to be an influence on them. My influence can either affect my children's future for their good or adversely. As parents, *as fathers,* we have this short window of time, and then we cut our children loose into adulthood. When I changed my thinking, I realized that I wasn't rearing children, I was rearing future fathers. If you want to know how you did as a parent see how your grandchildren turn out.

As fathers, we are given our children for an extremely short time. With some children, the time is shorter than others. In comparison to eternity, our time with our children is less than a blink of the eye.

Longing for a Father

> If you're not spending time with your children, someone else is.

I was talking with a friend recently who has two children. His children are the same ages as our son, Roman, and our daughter, Gabrielle. He was saying that everyone told him when his children were young to cherish every moment, for the moments would pass quickly and would soon be gone. He shared an observation with me. He said that when you're not sleeping for days, weeks, and for some parents, years, you can't imagine the time passing quickly! But then all of a sudden, the babies are sleeping and so are you; then they are going to school, then dating, graduating, and 'poof' they are gone! His wondering comment to me was, "What happened? Where did the time go?"

We must guard our time with our very lives, for it is fleeting, quickly dissipating right in front of our eyes. Our little ones grow up so fast, and we don't know where the time went. It was used up at work, in the yard, in front of the television, and sleeping! What little bit left was used to build relationships that mold and shape the lives of our little ones for a lifetime.

Our children deserve more than our leftovers. Don't you think so? When all we have to give our children are the scraps of time left each day, then we will eventually reap what we sow. We want our children to have fruitful lives and we definitely want to be a huge part of that fruit in our long-term relationships as parents, but if what we give them is the seed for the harvest of our future we may want to rethink the quantity and the quality of those seeds planted early.

Many times we try to excuse our lack of time given to those we love by saying we give them quality time versus quantity time. Quantity to those we love is quality! Quantity is MORE TIME, and that equates to quality in the mind and lives of those receiving it. If the words and thoughts of your heart are that you have to make time to spend with your children, you are already defeated by the way you think. Time spent with loved ones cannot be a *have to* kind of thing. It is a *want to* heart and mindset.

You don't make time; you TAKE time with your children. Taking time is an investment of your life into their lives. What do you expect from an investment? Well, of course, if you are smart at all, you expect an investment to give you back a return! Investing in your children's lives gives you a future return in your own life!

Time has no exact value. That's why it's priceless.

If you are the type of person who thinks memories and good times revolve around money, think again! If you think, "I don't have the money to do anything exciting with them," you need to rethink your relationship. When our children were young we went to the park on Saturday mornings and played on the swing sets. Now our children are grown men, and still even as I am writing this, Roman is pacing back and forth outside my office door. What does he want? He wants me, Dad, to go to the park and play basketball with him! What a concept! It costs me nothing but my attention and my time. What a huge harvest!

These were great memories when the children were small and even now, and they cost me nothing monetarily. We spent time, sometimes, only minutes or half an hour throwing the football, or the baseball, but the value of what was created, cannot be measured.

I even loved playing Barbies with Gabrielle. Cheryl only had one Barbie when was a little girl. So when I would buy one Barbie for Gabrielle, I also bought one for Cheryl. So there were plenty to go around. Today I still can't walk down a Barbie aisle in a toy store because of all those memories. Don't get me wrong, playing with Gabrielle was a good memory, but her not being with us here on earth anymore is still extremely difficult. I try to steer clear of the separation memories so as not to provoke the hurt. In that way, most of the time, I can then reflect on the fun and happy times without the pain of the visual reminder.

Time is the one thing that connects seed to harvest.

SEED-TIME-HARVEST.

Quite simple to see and even to understand, so we must not minimize it. Time is our friend, not our enemy. **Time is of great value when treasured and of great price when squandered.** We cannot get back what is behind us, but we can make choices today to change our thinking, our priorities, and our futures.

> Time is of great value when treasured and of great price when squandered.

I have said to our sons for years, "Show me your friends, and I will show you your future." Here might be a better way to personally apply that school of thought. "Show me how much time you are willing to spend with your children when they are young, and I will show you how much time they are willing to spend with you when you are old."

Longing for a Father

Here is a little test I call the dash-mark test. When my father died, the Marine Corps provided a marker for his grave as a marine veteran. On the marker was his name, date of birth, and the words: MARINE, SON, HUSBAND, FATHER. I went back to his grave as an adult and noticed something about the grave marker. Etched in stone was the day my father was born and the day he died, but between those dates was a dash mark, a simple one-inch line so very small and seemingly insignificant. But I realized that one-inch dash mark represented my father's whole life. One inch represented 43 years of life. And in that one inch were all the things my father did and the accomplishments and the memories he created. I thought he was a marine, a son, a successful businessman, and a father. But when I was trying to expound on the father part and the memories, it hit me. I couldn't tell you how much money he made in his lifetime, or how many battles he was in during the war or what type of son he was. The only things I could recall were the father/son memories. I thought it would take me a long time to process them but to my surprise it didn't take that long.

Actually, for a man who lived 43 years, my memories of my father were very few. And then this question hit me. What will my dash mark represent to my sons one day, should the Lord tarry? Fame, finances, houses, cars, or stories that they can recall of the times we spent together as father and sons? Take the dash-mark test in your life now. It's never too late to take inventory of your life. If you don't like who you are, it's time to change, and it's never too late to change.

> Where is your treasure? That's where you'll find your heart.

There is no doubt about it. It's not easy to have enough time. In fact, you will never have enough time; you have to take the time. But where do I get the time to take? *Take the time from other things.* Where is your treasure? That's where you'll find your heart.

You had enough time to buy the clothes you are wearing right now. You had enough time to get a haircut, which is still one of our favorite things to do together as father and sons. It's a big joke to our sons to get haircuts with me as my hair is not nearly as thick as theirs. What's the joke? That I never seem to get my money's worth and that God is so good to me that He made the word 'hair' mean both plural and singular! My boys are funny with their ol' dad! We go and have a great time together. And no, it's not that I pay for the haircuts, it's because we do it together! Of course, I never really thought about it before but maybe they are so happy to still be going out together to get haircuts because they are so happy that I am no longer cutting their hair like I did when they were little! I had no idea how bad a barber I was until we looked at some old photos and the boys said, "Dad, didn't you like us???" We had a big laugh over that one. I just loved being with them. I thought it was something fathers and sons did together. My dad never did it with me, but Andy Griffith always did it with Opie, didn't he?

The other day I took Roman to get a haircut. Afterwards he said, "Dad, let's get a bite of lunch together." We did and when the ticket came to pay he grabbed it and said, "Dad, this is my treat." I told him that he didn't have to do that, but he insisted as he said, "I don't have to, Dad. I want to! I want to bless you for all the times you have blessed me!" Are your children an investment or an expense? I am now beginning to reap a return on my investment in my sons. I laughed and reminded Roman that I bought him his first car... I can't wait for that return!

Be careful what you sow because you will reap it. We went to the barber recently and the boys were telling the woman how I wanted my hair cut, she spoke very little English and was fluent in Spanish. I don't speak any Spanish but the boys have some understanding. I didn't know what they were saying but when the woman was done I realized I was the butt-end of the boys' joke that day. Instead of telling the woman I wanted a little cut off (un poquito) they said leave un poquito. I mean to tell you that all those bad haircuts I gave them came home to roost in one haircut! We got home and walked into the house and Cheryl said, "What did you do to your hair?" I didn't even get a word out because the two boys were on the floor laughing and Cheryl knew there was something they needed to tell her! Well, you know the story... what you sow you will reap. From now on I will be paying closer attention not only to the barber but to my two jokesters of sons.

Roman, Dad and Harry III

Chapter Three

The Value of Time

I read a story about a man who spent time every morning with God in a particular room in his home. God was very pleased with the man when he gave Him his time. The man grew in his relationship with God. Then the man got more successful in life. He got married and had children. His job began to demand more of his time and energy. His family needed his attention too. Little by little, his routine of meeting with God each morning began to be interrupted and each day, the time spent seemed to grow less and less. The man felt guilty as he passed the room, looking inside all too briefly only to catch a glimpse of his once intimate meeting place. After a while the man didn't even bother looking in the room where he had met God early each morning. He would walk past the doorway quickly and not even glance toward the special meeting place.

Then one day the man realized how much he missed his time alone with God. He could not pass the room where they had met any longer. He went to meet with God and to say how much he missed his time with Him. God replied, "You think you miss Me? What you don't realize is when you chose to engage in things other than our time together, I still came to meet you. Why would I do that?

Because I miss you! I long to be with you more than you need to be with Me."

> Our children long to be with us even more than we need to be with them!

When we get too busy to be with our children, they miss us. They miss being with us! At least for a season of their lives, they miss their time with us. There is a definite time in our children's lives when hanging with Dad is really cool. While that time is available and our children want to be with us, we need to be investing our time in them.

Our time with our children is like seed being planted in their lives. While the conversation may not be stimulating, the abundant amount of love being unconditionally poured upon us can be overwhelming!

When our children are little they want our time, and our attention. We need to invest that time in them. It can produce a return of great proportions. If we do not give them the time when they are little, we may wake up one morning and realize they are not around. All of a sudden, when they no longer want our attention or our time, that's when we want their time and attention even more.

I've heard parents say that, "Just when my kids began to be fun to be around they were gone!" Your perception of your children at a young age could be the mirror-image of how they perceive you at an old age! If all you do is tolerate your children while they are young, it could be that all they do with you when you are old is tolerate you!

> If you just 'tolerate' your children when they are young, don't be surprised if they just 'tolerate' you when you are old.

We are given a short period of time to influence our children and I look at it this way. It's like when my wife and I go out to a speaking engagement. We've learned to never give them all you know. Always leave them wanting you to do more, say more, continue on even further. It's important as a speaker to always leave them wanting more and desiring for you to return again later. As fathers, we should give our children our time and energy in their early developing years, so as they grow up and become teens, they will want to spend more and more time with Dad! Our time spent with our children in their early years gives them a taste for our relationship to grow. When they become teens they are much more likely to want us around because they have a confidence in our relationship, and an expectation that we are available and present for them. They have a 'taste' for us in their lives. As the book of Proverbs states, *"...despise not your mother when she is old."* (Proverbs 23:22, AMP)

Our sons are past teenagers now, but they still want papa time. They know I am not a video game player but they take the time to teach me several different games, usually sports, so we can play them together. It does not really matter what we do together; they just want me with them. And our boys want their individual time with me. Never in your life have you ever met two more different men as our two sons, but both wonderful, godly men.

Harry III loves wrestling, UFC fights, and these types of things. Roman loves basketball, watching it and playing it. I give them my best now, all that I can muster up, I give it. We go to sporting events, we watch them together on TV, we hit the court and play ball together... I want them to have more memories than their minds can hold. I want them to have so many stories of their times with Dad that their kids will say, "Okay Dad, enough with the stories!"

I've seen the bumper stickers that say, "Real Men Love Jesus." And yes, they do! But I'd like to

Real Men Love Jesus... and Real Happy Men Love their Kids!

expand that statement to read, "Real Men Love Jesus... and Real Happy Men Love their Kids."

If you are an attorney you may get $500.00 an hour because the world puts that value on your time. There are athletes today who are getting paid because of the value placed on their athletic ability. Some football players are making 32 million dollars for one football season – that's 16 games. That equals out to paying them 2 million dollars a game! If they play 60 actual minutes, that is equal to $2,000,000.00 an hour! Is anyone really worth that kind of money? But something is only worth what someone else is willing to pay for it!

Jesus valued you and me and paid the price of our redemption with His life. God wanted a family so badly that He created you and me. We messed up as a human race so much that we were no longer a part of the family that He longed for and created. So what did He do? He valued a Father/child relationship with humanity for eternity so much, He paid the price of His only begotten Son, Jesus' life. His Son paid for our way to be bought back into the family of God. Has anyone ever paid your way on a trip? Has anyone ever bought you a plane ticket for you to go on a trip? Jesus paid the ultimate price for your ticket to heaven, into eternity with Him, so that we could be reunited with Him for eternity. Now try to put a value on that!

So as an example of a father/son relationship of love, what price, or value are you willing to pay to have a relationship with your family? Have you ever seen the movie, "Home Alone"? In the story, the family flew off for a Christmas vacation and left one of the sons alone at home. Once they realized it, the mother did everything possible, and even what others would have said was impossible to get back to be with her son. She left the entire family, her husband, and all her other children in France, to make her way back to her son left behind in Chicago. She went through what seemed to her like hell to get back to him. But in the movie there was an old man who lived next door. He was misunderstood by all the neighborhood children. They thought he was evil and mean. They didn't know him at all. They just judged him because of what they thought they saw in his life.

This old man had a family, a son, but because of things that had been said between them, the father and son had no relationship. After several scenes in the movie we find the old man and the young boy who has been left alone sitting side by side in church listening to the young choir sing Christmas songs. As the old man talked to the young boy, the old man realized his part in the brokenness of the relationship. The young boy said, "I wouldn't let anything come between my family and me especially at Christmas. Why don't you call your son?" The old man said that he didn't know if the son would talk to him or not. The little boy basically said, "What have you got to lose?" Because the old man was so afraid of rejection from his son, he had already predicted his future by doing nothing! The little boy made the simplest and yet most profound statement, "Well, at least you would know!" Think about it. What have you got to lose or fear? Call your father, or your son, or your daughter. Call that loved one you have lost relationship with over... what does it really matter what it was over? The only thing that matters is that the relationship has been lost and you should do your part in the restoration if possible. At least you would know!

If you have a problem with someone in your family the Bible says in Matthew 5:23-25, *"Therefore if you bring your gift to the altar, and there remember that your brother has something against you, leave your gift there before the altar, and go your way. First be reconciled to your brother, and then come and offer your gift. Agree with your adversary quickly, while you are on the way with him, lest your adversary deliver you to the judge, the judge hand you over to the officer and you be thrown into prison."*

This is a simple little parable, or story in the Bible saying that making peace with those around us is our responsibility. It does not say that we will always be able to do so, but that we should always make the first step. We understand that if we have a problem with someone else, but this verse tells us that if they have a problem with us we should go to them and try to work it out.

I Thessalonians 5:13 says, *"...Be at peace among yourselves."*

Mark 9:50 states, *"Salt is good, but if the salt loses its flavor, how will you season it? Have salt in yourselves, and have peace with one another."*

Romans 12:18 says it best, *"If it is possible, as much as depends on you, live peaceably with all men."*

No one realizes more than me that sometimes it is not possible to be in deep relationship with everyone you love. But when it is possible, *as much as depends on me,* ah, there it is! My part is to do what I can to live peaceably with those around me. Let's all say it together. "It's not about me!" When you have tried to work it out and it still has not changed on their part, well at least you know!

Keeping our own hearts and minds clear is the biggest job of all. I can't be trying to keep everyone else's life cleaned up because taking care of my own heart, mind, and life is a full time job. When it's possible, as far as I am concerned, I will live at peace with all people. I'm not saying this is easy but anything worth having is worth paying a price for. Sometimes, family and friends are separated by distance. Not to worry... you can love from a distance.

Even more important than our relationship with people, is our relationship with the Father God. Think about this, when we go to the Son of God, because we are out of relationship with the Father, He forgives us, and opens the door; He is the door (John 10:7) for us to come back in the most precious of all relationships. Do you need to go to the Father God and reestablish your relationship with Him? It's up to you. He has already paid the price for you. He has already bought your ticket. He has already purchased your fare. You just need to do one simple thing. Just talk with Him. He is always listening. What do you have to lose?

Do you need to go to the Father God and reestablish your relationship with Him?

Chapter Four

Children: Investment or Expense?

I learned very early that young boys need the influence of real men in their lives. Our oldest son Harry III was a tough, solid and rough kid. He got up early and now I realize it was because he wanted to see me leave each morning. It was important to him to tell me goodbye each day.

Cheryl usually had the children waiting for me when I got home each night. We spent time together, having meals, watching their kids' movies together, etc. each night. Roman came into our lives and for every rough and tough bone in Harry, Roman was tender, kind, loving and sweet. When Harry wanted to wrestle and slug me, Roman wanted to sit close to me and hug me. I had to learn to be to my boys what they needed, not what I wanted to give.

Roman, as a young boy, would tend to sleep late, and as I said earlier, Harry would get up early. Usually on Saturday mornings, I would have my list of chores, and projects to get accomplished that weekend. As I would head out the door to the hardware store or somewhere else where testosterone would be flowing Harry was always ready to go.

Longing for a Father

I remember one particular day when Roman was about four years old. I got up early. Harry was dressed and ready to go with Dad and off we went to the store to do guy things. When we returned home, Roman was standing at the back door with his little fists on his waist. He was so mad at me! Cheryl told me the whole story.

Right after Harry and I had gone out the back door, Roman had dragged his sleepy little head into the kitchen. He had asked his mama of the whereabouts of his dad and brother. When she told him that we had left on an errand, he was so upset. She said he stomped all the way down the little back hallway to the back door, and stood there absolutely furious. She said he literally shouted at the door as if I were standing there, **"You left me with the women!"**

To this day this is a saying we have between us men in the home, whether it's me being left or one of the boys. **"You left me with the women!"** This means, "Hey, what about me! Did you forget something? Namely, me!!!"

Of course, that was the cutest thing Cheryl had ever seen, so she promptly broke out in laughter at him, which did not diminish his anger at his father! He stood there for over an hour, getting madder by the minute. By the time we returned home, he had rehearsed his little line over and over. We came through the back door and all he could say over and over was, "Daddy, you left me with the women!"

Even for a four-year-old little boy, his daddy time was important. It may be even more important than we can ever know.

Our children are an investment. What do we expect our investments to do? We expect them to grow, to mature, to increase and gain momentum, to become more than they were at the beginning. When we have the mentality that our children are an investment, we will have a different attitude toward our time with them.

As long as we see our children as an expense, then that is what they will be to us their entire lives. It is not what they are, but what we perceive that they are. Therefore in our lives, they never become more, rather they become less.

►An expense diminishes; an investment increases.

►An expense is a negative; an investment is a positive.

►An expense is in the minus column; an investment is in the plus column.

►Children are not an expense; children are an investment for our future.

I saw a t-shirt recently that said, "Jesus: The First Blood Donor." Now that is a true statement, and that was an investment that is still paying dividends today!

One of the most obvious time investments I have seen a great return on is during the Christmas season. Ever since our children were little, well, it actually started with our very first Christmas together as a family. Cheryl and I got married on Friday before Mothers' Day. We got pregnant on the July 4th holiday weekend, and right before our first anniversary our first son, Harry III, was born on March 21st. He was only nine months old when our first Christmas together began and I was all ready!

Just as little girls spend their lives dreaming of their wedding day, I had spent my life dreaming of my Christmases as a father with my children. I had planned it all out in my head. From our first Christmas, with Lil' Harry, I bought more gifts than we could put in the Christmas tree room. I put a beautiful candy trail from the bedroom of our nine-month-old son to the Christmas tree. There was a bag for the candy waiting at his door for him to retrieve all the Christmas goodies on his way to the tree.

I would stay up late the night before, Christmas Eve, putting all the toys together. Cheryl would laugh at me and say on Christmas morning, "I slept so well last night," as she knew full well that I had only a few hours sleep. I would say to her, "You didn't stay up and help me." She would quickly answer back, "I wouldn't have waited until Christmas Eve to do all the work!"

Women just don't get it. It's a guy thing to wait until Christmas Eve and put all the toys together! Part of the excitement and the challenge was doing all that assembling the night before the big event. It's our challenge and our accomplishment!

As I look back over it all, I realize now that the candy trail was the greatest of all ideas. Because I had very little sleep as the children bounded from their beds screaming that Santa had actually come, the candy trail would slow them down enough to give me time to get up, wash my face, throw on my pajama bottoms, grab the video camera and hardly miss a beat! Great idea, huh?

As each child was born, the candy trail grew from one doorway to another. Like branches on a tree my candy trail would wander off in each direction at the top of the stairs to each precious little room. A bag of appropriate color would be waiting for each child. A pink or bright purple bag for the princess, Gabrielle, and blue and green bags for the young princes!

They would screech and scream their excited little phrases, each precious in themselves, as we watched in wonder as they so selflessly sorted through which candy was meant for each child. How precious to hear Harry III, standing over a particular kind of candy that he knew was Roman's favorite as he proclaimed boldly to his brother in his not yet lost little speech issue, "Woeman (that stood for Roman in Harry III speech!), Santa left this candy for you!" And of course, Roman would answer back over the very next piece of candy on the carpet, "Hawwy (which of course, meant Harry in sweet Roman's vocabulary) this one is for you!"

Then when Gabrielle came onto the ever anticipated candy trail, each one went through the much awaited ritual of retrieving every tiny bit of sweet delicious markers ever pointing forward to the pot at the end of the rainbow... THE CHRISTMAS TREE! Of course, there was actually no means to access the tree as I had piled the room with so many presents, wrapped and unwrapped until the floor of the room was so covered in prizes that it literally took a couple hours to approach the base of the tree!

I invested in them with time, love, effort, and money. It was my honor and privilege to do this each and every year. It was the most exciting and fun time of my entire year. After Gabrielle crossed over to heaven, I just could not bring myself to do it anymore. Our sons were still quite small. Harry III was twelve and Roman was nine years old that first Christmas. Gabrielle had only been gone for a month that first Christmas. I just could not do it. We tried; Cheryl tried, everyone tried but it was so hard.

The next Christmas the boys were thirteen and ten years old and still I just could not find the strength to do my famous candy trail. When we awakened Christmas morning to the sound of the boys stirring around our bed there was an excitement with the children I had not known for months.

They wanted us to get up, and get up now! They were making happy sounds, hurrying us up to come and see what Santa had done for us. As we rose out of bed, I put on my pajama bottoms and slippers, and rubbed my sleepy eyes as I walked toward the doorway of our bedroom. The boys were jumping up and down, clapping their little hands together and actually giggling!

When I finally got the sleep rubbed out of my eyes, it was immediately replaced by huge tears. There in our bedroom doorway were two bags, one pink for Mama, and one blue for me. Immediately following the bags was a trail of candy from our bedroom doorway, down the hall, down the steps, and into the Christmas tree room. Each step I took, I cried a little more; these were happy tears for a change.

Now over ten years later, a different house, in a different state... still two bags sitting at our bedroom door on Christmas morning and the biggest and best candy trail leading to the Christmas tree! I invested in them, now Harry has taken it upon himself, along with Roman, to do it for us. They do it together. He somehow, even as a young teenager, used his own money to buy the candy that he knew were his Mama and Daddy's favorites. He waited until we went to bed and fell asleep and he gave us the reward of all rewards. He reminded us that life indeed goes on.

It's a tradition in our home and I believe it will be a tradition in both their homes and families as they grow as fathers in their lives. I planted it in their lives. I showed them how to do it unselfishly, now I receive it each and every Christmas as a harvest in our lives through our children.

Chapter Five

It's Not What I Did; It's What I Didn't Do

I am the youngest of three children, and the only boy. I didn't have *a* mother, I had *three* mothers. My mom and both my sisters mothered me until our father died. Then people said I had to become the man of the house. When we lose something as a child, we tend to spend much of our adult life trying to retrieve it. I lost my boyhood – my childhood. I wanted to be a boy, but boyhood was lost for me. I came to realize I could not go back and do it again, nor could I retrieve those years that were gone, on my own.

> It was not years I was longing for, it was *relationship*.

What could I do to find the fulfillment of a lost childhood? I had to learn and recognize that it was not years I was longing for... it was relationship. I missed a father/son relationship. That was what I was longing for, that was the void in my life.

When our first son, Harry III, was born, I cried. Tears ran down this face where tears had seldom been. I had my own "Kunta Kinte moment," where I held my infant son, my firstborn, up to God, symbolizing, "Yes! I did it. Here he is," as he proceeded to pee all over me.

My heart was so full because I felt that God had answered my prayers to restore my father/son relationship. My earthly father was not coming back to the earth, but I had become the father to a wonderful son.

> I wanted to give my son everything that I did not have as a child, but what he needed the most was my time.

I wanted everything for our son that I could not have. I wanted him to know my love, understand my heart of giving towards him. I wanted him to experience my presence, by simply being in his life. I thought my intentions were admirable, noble, and honorable. But my actions were more dictated by my environment and expectations of a heavy work schedule, than by the desire of my heart to always be there for our son.

I wanted Harry to fulfill the obvious purpose of his creation. He was tall, barrel-chested, and a big boy! It was quite apparent that he was going to play sports, probably football by the way he was naturally built. I had him in every sport allowed for his age. His first real team sport was t-ball and I expected him to be the best ball player ever born. After all, he had all the right natural equipment, plus he was my son, and I was great at every sport! He was built like a catcher and he threw right-handed and batted left. Just think of it, a left-handed catcher; his ticket to the major leagues! And he has blue eyes. I once heard that blue-eyed people pick the baseball up sooner when batting than brown-eyed people. He had it all!

I remember going to one of his first games and noticing that the coach had put him in the outfield. I could not believe my eyes! This heavy-hitter should be perfectly placed in the lineup and he should be playing catcher for sure! I was disappointed, but tried to encourage Harry and not show my feelings. My thoughts were, "Once they see Harry with his outstanding skills in the outfield they'll bring him in and put him at catcher where he belongs or at least at first base where all the action is!"

When the team hit the field, Harry was the last one out on the field. While the other boys were running to their positions on the field Harry was, well, at best, he was strolling. I yelled to him to get a move on, to show some excitement, to hustle! Harry just looked over at me, gave me a big grin and a little wave and kept tiptoeing through the grass.

Needless to say, I was exasperated with him. But that was not the end of it, oh no! When the ball did come his way in the outfield, he was anything but ready for it! He seemed to be inspecting the blades of grass, and looking for four-leaf clovers throughout the entire game. When a ball did wind up in his hands, which was a true miracle, he didn't even know where to throw it back into the infield. I just could not believe my eyes! Not my boy!

When we got home after the game, I was beside myself. I was exasperated, walking back and forth in the kitchen, asking what in the world was wrong with this boy? What got into him? I said to Cheryl, "Why didn't he do what he knew to do? Why? He acted like he doesn't even know how to throw the ball!"

It's not what I did, it's what I didn't do.

She looked me straight in the face and said, "Well, he doesn't know how to throw the ball."

I reacted quite loudly with, "What? What are you talking about? Of course, he knows how to throw the ball!"

Cheryl asked me the most profound question, "How is he supposed to know how to throw the ball? Did you teach him? Have you worked with him?"

I was stopped dead still in my tracks. I didn't know what to say. All I could think was that he must have been born knowing how to throw the ball! It was not what I did, but what I didn't do that dawned on me that day. Not having my father around me I thought that I had learned all by myself how to throw a baseball. But that wasn't all true. My dad did show me when I was very young but I had forgotten. I was so focused on what I didn't have after ten-years-old that I forgot what I did have before my father died.

It was a devastating realization that I had actually failed in my job as Dad. The very thing I had spent years saying I would do, I hadn't done. I had assumed he would be great at sports but I had never spent any time teaching him. After that great awakening, I spent more time working with him, training and teaching him the art of throwing, catching, and hitting the ball.

But no matter how much we practiced, sports were not his thing. We tried baseball, and not for a year or two, but for six years, from t-ball through the top years of little league, but he never loved it. I think he simply did it for me. We played basketball at the YMCA, did the basketball team sports, and even Taekwando, but no matter how much we tried to help Harry be great at sports, he simply did not enjoy them.

When I looked at Harry, I saw sports, all sports, and especially football, but he never even wanted to try football. He was built like a linebacker. That's what I saw when I looked at him. But the way he was built had not designed the inside of his character.

He was much more interested in the Three Tenors than he was in Babe Ruth. He was gifted alright. There was no way around that, but it was not in sports. He was smart, a true and amazing reader. He loved to read! He could watch an educational video, and without our even realizing it, he had the entire script memorized.

Cheryl read to him day after day, hour after hour. He had a huge thirst for knowledge. If he heard it, he had it memorized. He could quote back to you things you had said word for word, and it had looked like he wasn't even listening when you were talking!

One day Harry came to me and announced that he was going to sing the national anthem at a college basketball game. It was his first show of any interest in sports! But not exactly what I had in mind.

I was amused at his little face, and his matter-of-factness about such an undertaking. In fact, I didn't even realize at the time that he could sing! He was about five years old or so, and with all the seriousness I could muster I told him that for such a task he would have to audition. He looked me square in the face and said, “I can do that.” After a long pause, he said, “Daddy, what is ‘audition’?” I explained that he would have to go in front of the person in charge of choosing who sings the anthem at the ball games and he would have to sing for him. He thought about it for a minute or two and he said, “Okay, I can do that.”

I didn’t want to burst his bubble, so I gently said, “Harry, the national anthem is a very difficult song to sing. Do you know the words?” Actually, I was thinking, “You don’t even know how to sing!” He confidently said, “Mama will teach me.” And she did, and he did.

Within a few weeks, he learned the entire national anthem, and with the biggest voice you have ever heard come out of a child, he sang the national anthem to a full ten thousand seat arena. He brought the house down without a doubt. Even the announcers were stunned and could not go on without commenting on the gift of this young boy.

He was so cute. He wore a suit and tie and walked out in the center of the arena. He grabbed the microphone and let it rip! No intimidation, no fear, not a care in the world. And when he was finished, he put the microphone down, walked back to courtside, pulled two GI Joes out of his pocket as if to say, “I’m done with that. Now it’s time to play.” He was a natural at singing and he was comfortable in that environment. It was second nature to him. I thought, “How can this be?” But then I remembered his mama is a natural musician and a great singer and she had done it since she was a little girl. Harry wasn’t just my son, he was our son and that gift came from his mama, not me. In fact, when Cheryl and I were talking about our young son preparing for this big performance, she remarked that she hoped that he would have ‘perfect pitch.’ I was confused about why she was making a baseball reference during this conversation, but I went along with her and replied, “Shoot, I just hope he can **hit** the ball!”

Harry III’s gift has always been music.

I learned during this experience, that as a parent **we cannot know the destiny and future of our children.** We cannot judge their outcome by their appearance and we most certainly can't predict what they are created to do and be. Harry to this day looks like a linebacker. He's six feet two inches, 225 pounds. But he is a researching, book-devouring, and thought-provoking singer, preacher, and writer. He's not a sissy, that's for sure. I don't even think about wrestling him as he found a love for weightlifting. He will hurt me with very little effort! But his gifts and callings are within him and have been from before he was born.

God puts greatness in a child. Fathers help pull it out of them.

I am learning to never assume anything of anyone. God has a plan and purpose and usually we don't know it. We will though, in time, so don't limit God, or your children. Don't assume an outcome by the way it looks; I have learned nothing is hardly ever as it looks!

Most of the time, there is more to a person than meets the eye. Harry proved that to me, that's for sure. When I began to realize this about our son, I began to realize it about myself, too. Maybe there was more to me than what I saw in the mirror also.

Longing for a Father

I like the movie, "Miracle," about the 1980 Olympic hockey team. I bought the DVD, and within the scenes they had an interview with the actual coach who was portrayed in the movie. The conversation went on between the coach, Herb Brooks, and the actor who portrayed him, Kurt Russell. In the interview, Kurt asked Coach Brooks why he picked the players he wound up with as his team. It seemed there was some controversy between who the Olympic committee thought would be on the team and who the coach actually chose to be on the team. Coach Brooks said that he picked the guys that he saw greatness within. He went on to say that if he did his job correctly, he could pull the greatness that was within each player to the surface in each individual life, creating a team of greatness.

God has put greatness within all of us. There is greatness in all of our children, in us, in you, and in your children. Sometimes that greatness consists mainly of the verse in I John 4:4 which says, *"You are of God, little children, and have overcome them, because He who is in you is greater than he who is in the world."*

Once we realize that the greatness within us is actually God on the inside of us, we just need to have that greatness or gifting come out of us. Sometimes it's a coach, a music teacher, a friend, or a parent or family member. But wouldn't it be great if every father could recognize the greatness in his own children and be the one who pulled it out of them?

If I had done that in my son's life I could have saved him a lot of frustration, but it wasn't too late for him, and it isn't too late for you, either. I don't care if your children are five or twenty-five; you can recognize the gifting within them and accept what God has put within them. Notice what they are passionate about, listen to what they love, and support them in it, encourage them. Because just like we all want to hear those words from our heavenly Father one day, "Well done, My good and faithful servant," our children would love to hear that from us, their earthly fathers.

> I'd rather fail at something I love than succeed at something I hate.

I have purposed in my heart to encourage and exalt our sons in their passions and loves. It might not be what I think they would love or be interested in but as I say in my own life, "I'd rather fail at doing something I love than succeed at doing something I hate."

I pray that my sons find something they love and are passionate about and are successful in that pursuit. And I have purposed in my heart to do what I can to help them succeed to that end, and not hinder them in their pursuit of their dreams.

As for Roman, he was a tentative little boy. Cheryl called him her skirt-hider. But when he walked on a baseball field, he had it. But he didn't really enjoy it or have a passion for it either. So I learned from Harry III to not push him. But when Roman was about sixteen he began to show interest in sports and a love for them began to develop within him, especially basketball. He played baseball because he could play on the team and be a part of the group, which he loved because he is very social. But it wasn't his love. Roman loved basketball. He began to work at his game and sharpen his skills, practicing for hours on end. He was virtually learning the competitive part of the game from scratch. I realized that not having played competitive sports all those years he didn't know the nuances of the game, but I wasn't going to push him. I let him learn as he made the team as a junior, but seeing him not engage in the game frustrated me. He had the skills but just couldn't get competitive!

I tried to intimidate him into changing, reward him into changing, and I found out I was not trying to change his athletic ability or his skills, but I was trying to change his personality. I was trying to make him into me! (I guess I still had a lot to learn!) By his senior year I let him do it his way, and took the pressure off him. Roman grew into a fine basketball player and has grown into a fine young man. Watching him play sports was such a blessing to me, a true gift from God. When he played his last game I was more down than he was. But you know, something greater and more joy-filled than watching him play basketball competitively is the fact that now he and I still play today against each other. We have a common love, not for the competition, but for the camaraderie. It's something we can do together as a father and son and that is more valuable and rewarding to me than any competitive game he ever played. He found his love for the game and together we have the enjoyment of doing it together.

Roman and Dad, on the last day of basketball, Roman's senior year in High School.

We are proud of our boys in all they do. God has placed diverse gifts and talents in them both.

Roman and Dad, on the last day of baseball, Roman's senior year in High School.

Harry III, helping lead worship at the We Who Worship Conference in 2010.

Chapter Six

Seeing Myself as God's 'Only' Child

As I mentioned earlier there was a movie made about the 1980 American Olympic Hockey team. The team was being coached by Herb Brooks. When the tryouts were held, Herb picked his team, but left what the experts thought were the best players off the team. He was severely questioned about how he chose the team, and that of course, made those in charge challenge his ability to coach the team as well. They invited the best players in America, gathering them all in one location so they could evaluate them easier and pick the most talented players to configure the best team possible.

But Coach Brooks explained that the 'best' players had been chosen time and time again, but to no avail in the gold medal department. The 'best' had been unable to put the American team in the win column. He explained to his superiors that anyone could see the physical greatness of the 'best' athletes but he believed that as the coach his job was not just to pick those which he saw greatness within. He believed his job was to see the greatness within each one, and pull that greatness out of them as a team. Great individuals did not always make a great team. The job of the coach was to find players, and pull them together as a team, and together develop that greatness as a team and fulfill the dream of America winning Olympic gold in hockey. They met much adversity, but when the final whistle sounded, America won the gold.

I believe each one of us has greatness within us. Maybe no one has ever seen it in you. Maybe no one has ever pulled upon the greatness within you. Maybe you don't even realize the greatness is there, but I assure you, there is greatness within you. I didn't have a father who told me I was great when I was a little boy, but I learned how to be a father who tells his children how great and wonderful they are. I have learned how to celebrate the unique gifts and talents within each one of our children and I am not shy about telling them either.

My wife, Cheryl, has greatness within her, and unlike most people, she knew it at an early age. She knew early in her life that she had a destiny for greatness and with a determined focus like none I have ever known, she discovered it, and eventually walked in it. Yes, she knew what she was to be, and she spent her life going after it.

I think I was more like most people in life... I just could not imagine anything about me being great. I could not imagine what I was to do and be, and even when God sent people in my life to tell me, to encourage me, I was so used to only hearing the 'bad things,' I had a deaf ear to the destiny-talkers in my life.

Once I was in a chapel and I jokingly stood up on the platform in the pulpit and kind of like a little boy said, "Mom, look at me!" I was making a joke, being sarcastic at my own expense, as if to say, "I could never stand in the pulpit of God."

But you see, my mom had dedicated me to God at birth... and getting me here was no easy task. My mother had a very difficult time during childbirth. Regarding that day I joked about my 'unworthiness' to stand in the pulpit of God, she told me later on that at the moment she looked up and saw me standing there, the Lord spoke to her heart and told her that was my destiny and that I would be speaking and ministering to people from His pulpit. It's probably a good thing she didn't tell me at the time, because I would not have heard her. In fact, I would have probably run from it as quickly and as far away as possible.

Later on, after I married Cheryl, she began faithfully praying for me. She knew I was not walking in my destiny and that I was not fulfilled. She wanted to talk about it, but I hardly ever would discuss it with her. I felt she would be disappointed in me, as I was disappointed in myself but truly I didn't know what I was supposed to be doing.

Maybe down deep inside my heart I knew, but I had closed that door long before I met Cheryl.

But no matter how many times I slammed the door on this conversation with her, she would continually come back to this door and knock, knock, knock. One day I was tired of talking to her about this and I made the horrible mistake of saying to her, "I guess I have settled with the life I have now."

Was this the poorest choice of words I could ever use!? "Settled," she said. "You are telling me that you have settled for less than God's best?" Well, I started back-pedaling trying to get out of the muddy water I was in by this point, but it was too late.

She proceeded to tell me that she would not let me 'settle.' Settling was not an option. She said, **"Settling means you know there is more, but you are unwilling to do what it takes to get to the 'promised land' in your personal life."** Oh, how I wished I had not opened that can of worms! But I could not take it back.

> "Settle"
> is a four-letter word.
>
> -Cheryl Salem

She pushed, and probed, and questioned to the point of making me so upset at times. She got inside my head, and then proceeded to swing wide the door of my heart. Quite frankly, she messed with me and would not leave me alone about it. If she wasn't talking to me about it, she was talking to God about it!

The more she prayed the more 'unsettled' I became. I had been unsatisfied all my life, but I had learned to live unsatisfied. Now that she had pointed it out and made a big deal about it, I could not simply shut the door on it again.

The Lord began dealing with my unresolved emotional issues. He began pulling up on the scab of my heart in the area of 'no dad.' He began causing me unrest in areas that I had put to bed long ago! He caused me to notice things I didn't want to notice, and see things I didn't want to see.

> Bringing a problem without a solution is just *complaining.*

One night, I could not sleep, so I was downstairs trying to get my mind to shut off so I could go to sleep. I was staring at the television but not really watching it. I had seen things in my life, things that others did, and said, that were not right. I had began to actually care about wrong, and injustice, and unrighteousness. But what did I do? I began to complain about it! I complained to Cheryl, to my friends, and mostly to the Lord. I didn't pray, I complained!

Finally, on that fateful night in front of the television as I was watching someone with a national platform speaking into people's lives, I once again began complaining to the Lord that I knew that person was... blah, blah, blah. I know they don't live... blah, blah, blah. After my long discussion, the Lord interrupted me with these words, "If you don't like what you see and hear, then do something about it."

Don't do what you can, do what it takes.

I went on to say to the Lord, "Somebody ought to do... blah, blah, blah." And the Lord said, "Then why don't YOU do something about it?" It's amazing to me when we bring a problem to God, He always has the solution, but be careful because unknowingly part of the solution might just include us. I loved to tell people, "If you bring me a problem then bring me a solution with it, because if you don't, you're only complaining." My complaining in this instance exposed a problem I thought God didn't know or even have a solution for, but I now realize that in my speaking forth from my heart, not complaining, I was also bringing the solution to God. That solution was in the form of me submitting to the will of God in my life and letting him as my Father gently guide me into my destiny.

It was settled right then and there. I had to work through some details of life. I had to finish some things I had started in the natural realm, but my destiny was sealed that night on the couch. My Almighty Coach, Jesus Christ, had reached inside my heart and found greatness... and He began pulling it out.

Making a decision without all of the facts is just judgment.

Up until that night it was easy for me to point out what I thought about someone I really didn't know. I just assumed they were not what they appeared to be. I was skeptical and yes, even judgmental sometimes. I should have been asking myself, "How well do I really know that person?" But I didn't. Actually my discomfort about them was probably my own unhappiness about myself. And I should have been asking how well I knew myself. When we have limited information on someone else and still make a decision based on half the facts, that's judgment. And we are not supposed to judge others. But having all the facts about ourselves and 100% knowing there is something wrong and not doing something about it is laziness, or fear, or at best 'ignorance gone to seed' as my wife says! Even denial, because I was denying God to use me for His intended purpose for my life. We all need to stop asking God to help us fulfill our dreams and start asking Him to let us help Him fulfill His dream for us.

Having the knowledge that I was not fulfilling everything in my life and feeling a burning desire to do more, I later found out was actually the calling and purpose in my life that was inside me. So now that I had the feeling and understood what it was, it really didn't matter to me what other people were doing. What mattered to me was what I was going to do. It is written in our nation's Declaration of Independence that, "...But when a long Train of Abuses and Usurpations, pursuing invariably the same Object, evinces a Design to reduce them under absolute Despotism, it is their Right, it is their Duty, to throw off such Government, and to provide new Guards for their future Security."

> *Responsibility* is not a bad word!

Just what does that really mean to you and me? It means if there is something wrong, those who have the ability to take action, *have the responsibility* to take action. If we know something is wrong and we do something about it that's called taking responsibility. That's what real God-kind of fathers do. They take responsibility, and when possible, they change the course of history.

I had to take responsibility for my own life and not just make excuses for the things that went wrong in my life as my escape from doing what I knew was right.

> My definition of responsibility... taking action to correct something you know is wrong!

Call it apathy, laziness or just a give-up attitude, but finding out that the scars in my life didn't have to keep me from doing what I was supposed to do in my life was huge. They were the things that marked me in life and could give me the opportunity to accept them as part of the purpose of my life. Don't despise where you came from or what you have come through, because it's brought you where you are today. What we go through is for a purpose and if we can use those marked events, and yes, even those scars in our lives as launching points instead of obstacles then we won't need someone else to pull the greatness out of us. We will find it springing forth from us almost effortlessly. We won't see ourselves as scarred but uniquely marked by all the events in our lives.

Years later, after our daughter went to heaven, Cheryl and I were in a shoe store and she was going to buy me a pair of shoes for my birthday. There was a sign by the checkout counter that read, "Clergy 10% Off Today," Cheryl said we are not technically clergy but we are ministers and before she could finish, the woman said, "Yes, that includes you." She later said, "Besides I recognize you. I know who you are." I heard the conversation and I thought the woman was going to say, "You're Cheryl Prewitt, Miss America 1980," or even Cheryl Salem the singer, but to my surprise, she said, "You're Gabrielle's mom and dad." Wow, she told us of how she followed Gabrielle's story and prayed for her and our family. Later that day I thought, because of this tragedy or scar we bear in our lives we were known to someone, then I thought we were known for our faith too, and our testimony. Then it finally hit me. I was Gabrielle's father and because of the work and faith of our daughter, this woman knew me. And isn't that how it's supposed to be, that others on earth get to know our heavenly Father because of His earthly children and what they go through and their faith and testimonies? Life isn't always about 'me and mine,' but about who we can affect in life. And there is our purpose,

> Show people the heavenly Father, through the works of His children.

to let our Father in heaven be revealed to others by His sons and daughters so that He is known for what His son went through for all of us.

We are all created uniquely even while going through life's path differently than every other person on this planet. Talk about being 'special.' You are something that is rare, something that is one of a kind. That's who you are! You are one of a kind, rare, and special! You are unique and the apple of your Father's eye! (Zechariah 2:8)

You know, in the "Miracle" movie I referred to about the Olympic hockey team, the coach was trying to get the players to know one another, to become a team, and learn to play as one unit with one goal. They had to learn to operate as a whole, not individuals with individual goals. In the movie, the coach would ask them to say their names and who they were representing. Each player would say their name and who they were representing by identifying their state, their college or university. Finally, it came to a point in the story, where the coach was fed up with the players, their individual needs, and wants. It was at a point where he was watching two players talk about people they were watching in the stands and not thinking about the game. They were more concerned with what they were going to do after the game, than with the game itself. So at the end of the game the coach made them run 'Herbies,' what we would call 'suicides,' back and forth on the ice until they were exhausted, vomiting, and they turned the lights off in the building.

The assistant coach and the trainer were not in agreement with this kind of action, because they didn't understand why he was doing this. Coach Brooks alluded to the fact that some of the players were thinking about what they were going to do after the game, instead of thinking about what the team was doing during the game. The team still did not seem to get the point of this exercise, until one of the players, not prompted by the coach, but voluntarily on his own, yelled out and said, "My name is Mike Eruzione, and I play for the United States of America!"

The coach just stared at him. It was at this point, that the coach ended the exercise and the look on the assistant coach's face was, "I understand this now. We needed them to understand that they are not individuals playing for individual goals." This was bigger than any one individual person, and what they were representing was bigger than their home town or college or even family. They were representing the entire United States of America and everything and everyone that that stands for.

In an earlier scene, the head coach had said that NHL all-star teams never beat the Russians because they were individuals trying to beat a team. Now the coach had a team that understood they were not representing their college, their families, or themselves. They were representing something bigger. They were representing their country, their nation. That one statement from one player marked the team from that moment on; they got it. It was not about them individually, but collectively.

I realize that our lives are bigger than a game, and we represent something greater than ourselves. But without our uniqueness and individuality, even our quirks, we can be overwhelmed and think that we are just a speck going unnoticed in this world. We must realize that one person can change the world, impact a nation, and make a difference. It does not start with seeing the strength in the masses; it starts with seeing ourselves uniquely chosen and divinely created and special to our heavenly Father. It's not in thinking that we are His step-children, but knowing that when He looks at you and when He looks at me, He sees each of us as His only child at that moment. That gives you and me the special and intimate relationship with Him, ultimately moving from having a heavenly Father, to having an intimate relationship with One I can call Papa. Just like the hockey players got it in one statement, here's something I want you to remember "life isn't always about you but your life might be about who you can affect in life." Someone asked me if our daughter fulfilled her purpose and destiny in her short life (only 6 years)? It made me think and begin to question, so I asked a man who we were sitting under at that time as our pastor that question. He immediately answered with this, **"It's not how long you have on this earth that matters, but what matters is what you do with the time you have on this earth."** Don't waste your life thinking it's all about you, I believe it's about who you can affect through your life.

I am God's
only child!

Chapter Seven

Revealing My Greatest Need

After my dad died, I lived my life torn between wanting to be a little boy, like more ten-year-olds, and feeling the responsibility of being the man of the house for my mom. I built a huge wall around my heart so no one could hurt me. You would too, if your father had said on his death bed, "Don't trust anyone. Don't be a sucker for anyone and don't cry at my funeral." Having known those words and letting them affect me in every area of my life, I remember walking from my grandfather's house to the barber shop one day. I got a haircut and walked back to his house. I was about eleven years old and when I got home he said to me, "I thought you were going to get a haircut today." I said, "I did!" (I liked my hair longer then as it was the style and I just went for a trim.) My grandfather said, "You sure got suckered."

I turned around and went back out the door to the barbershop and got my $1.25 worth! I'll tell you that was a haircut! Now to try and explain to my friends why I had done what I did took some doing. But I had to prove that I did not get suckered by anyone, ever! I just called it my summer haircut!

When a teacher at school or a coach on a sports team would try to give me advice, I assumed they were not going to be there when I needed them and

I would not let them into my life. Of course, this also meant that I didn't listen to what they had to say, either. Most folks don't keep pouring into a life when the container has a lid on it!

Most folks don't keep pouring into a life when the container has a lid on it!

I was in high school and one day our team was playing baseball and when the game was over, we didn't have the desired outcome. We had just lost and I was upset. Losing never has come naturally to me. I don't believe losing *should* come naturally to us. We were born in the image of God and He is a winner only! He never loses.

One of the fathers of another player came over to me, and put his hand on my shoulder. He was trying to get me to calm down and not be so upset so he said, "Son, calm down. It's not that important. It's just a game." I turned to him and shoved his hand off my shoulder with these words, "I'm not your son!"

I had an attitude. My attitude said for everyone to leave me alone. It said, "Don't try to replace my dad! You can't! Don't even try!" Not only did I have a chip on my shoulder, as I got older it became more and more apparent. Everyone around me saw it, and if possible, I went around them trying to get them to knock it off! I didn't think I needed anyone else to help or advise me, nor did I want it. I thought that I didn't need anyone else. "I can do it by myself," was my motto. I was certain the only reason someone would want to help me was that they knew I would do what I set out to do and they just wanted to take part of the credit.

Even God seemed to be a threat to me and not trustworthy. I wouldn't let go and let God do or be anything for me. I thought, "I don't need to bother Him. He has more important things and more important people to help than me."

No matter how tough I tried to act, it didn't fill the void in my soul. I had a huge need and no one could fill it. I needed a father. I thought that need could never be filled because my dad had died. I blamed him for leaving me. I was angry because he was not in my life. I was mad at every boy whose father was still alive. And of course, I was buying the biggest lie of them all, "There is no one in the whole world who understands what I am feeling."

Father/son events, church events, camping events, awards banquets... it didn't matter what they called it, I wouldn't go, never! Ever! So like most hurt people, I shut down emotionally. I shut down my dreams, desires, and hopes. I shut down my ability to love and be loved. I closed the door and painted shut the window to my heart. I needed a father and there was no one who could meet that need... or so I thought.

My life was much like Gideon's in the Bible. Gideon's story is one of those that most of us guys can relate to. It is found in the book of Judges, chapter 6:11 and continues through chapter 7:25.

11Now the Angel of the Lord came and sat under the oak (terebinth) at Ophrah, which belonged to Joash the Abiezrite, and his son Gideon was beating wheat in the winepress to hide it from the Midianites.

12And the Angel of the Lord appeared to him and said to him, The Lord is with you, you mighty man of [fearless] courage.

13And Gideon said to him, O sir, if the Lord is with us, why is all this befallen us? And where are all His wondrous works of which our fathers told us, saying, Did not the Lord bring us up from Egypt? But now the Lord has forsaken us and given us into the hand of Midian.

14The Lord turned to him and said, Go in this your might, and you shall save Israel from the hand of Midian. Have I not sent you?

15Gideon said to Him, Oh Lord, how can I deliver Israel? Behold, my clan is the poorest in Manasseh, and I am the least in my father's house.

16The Lord said to him, Surely I will be with you, and you shall smite the Midianites as one man.

17Gideon said to Him, If now I have found favor in Your sight, then show me a sign that it is You Who talks with me.

18Do not leave here, I pray You, until I return to You and bring my offering and set it before You. And He said, "I will wait until you return."

19Then Gideon went in and prepared a kid and unleavened cakes of an ephah of flour. The meat he put in a basket and the broth in a pot, and brought them to Him under the oak and presented them.

20And the Angel of God said to him, Take the meat and unleavened cakes and lay them on this rock and pour the broth over them. And he did so.

21Then the Angel of the Lord reached out the tip of the staff that was in His hand, and touched the meat and the unleavened cakes, and there flared up fire from the rock and consumed the meat and the unleavened cakes. Then the Angel of the Lord vanished from his sight.

22And when Gideon perceived that He was the Angel of the Lord, Gideon said, Alas, O Lord God!

For now I have seen the Angel of the Lord face to face!

23The Lord said to him, Peace be to you, do not fear; you shall not die.

24Then Gideon built an altar there to the Lord and called it, The Lord is Peace. To this day it still stands in Ophrah, which belongs to the Abiezrites.

25That night the Lord said to Gideon, Take your father's bull, the second bull seven years old, and pull down the altar of Baal that your father has and cut down the Asherah [symbol of the goddess Asherah] that is beside it;

26And build an altar to the Lord your God on top of this stronghold with stones laid in proper order. Then take the second bull and offer a burnt sacrifice with the wood of the Asherah which you shall cut down.

27Then Gideon took ten men of his servants and did as the Lord had told him, but because he was too afraid of his father's household and the men of the city to do it by day, he did it by night.

28And when the men of the city arose early in the morning, behold, the altar of Baal was cast down, and the Asherah was cut down that was beside it, and the second bull was offered on the altar which had been built.

29*And they said to one another, Who has done
this thing? And when they searched and asked,
they were told, Gideon son of Joash has done this
thing.*

30*Then the men of the city commanded Joash,
Bring out your son, that he may die, for he has
pulled down the altar of Baal and cut down the
Asherah beside it.*

31*But Joash said to all who stood against him,
Will you contend for Baal? Or will you save him?
He who will contend for Baal, let him be put to
death while it is still morning. If Baal is a god, let
him contend for himself because one has pulled
down his altar.*

32*Therefore on that day he called Gideon
Jerubbaal, meaning, Let Baal contend against
him, because he had pulled down his altar.*

33*Then all the Midianites and the Amalekites and
the people of the east came together and, crossing
the Jordan, encamped in the Valley of Jezreel.*

34*But the Spirit of the Lord clothed Gideon with
Himself and took possession of him, and he blew a
trumpet, and [the clan of] Abiezer was gathered to
him.*

35*And he sent messengers throughout all
Manasseh, and the Manassites were called to
follow him; and he sent messengers to Asher, to*

Zebulun, and to Naphtali, and they came up to meet them.

36*And Gideon said to God, If You will deliver Israel by my hand as You have said,*

37*Behold, I will put a fleece of wool on the threshing floor. If there is dew on the fleece only and it is dry on all the ground, then I shall know that You will deliver Israel by my hand, as You have said.*

38*And it was so. When he rose early next morning and squeezed the dew out of the fleece, he wrung from it a bowlful of water.*

39*And Gideon said to God, Let not your anger be kindled against me, and I will speak but this once. Let me make trial only this once with the fleece, I pray you; let it now be dry only upon the fleece and upon all the ground let there be dew.*

40*And God did so that night, for it was dry on the fleece only, and there was dew on all the ground.*

Judges 7

1*THEN JERUBBAAL, that is, Gideon, and all the people who were with him rose early and encamped beside the spring of Harod; and the camp of Midian was north of them by the hill of Moreh in the valley.*

2The Lord said to Gideon, The people who are with you are too many for Me to give the Midianites into their hands, lest Israel boast about themselves against Me, saying, My own hand has delivered me.

3So now proclaim in the ears of the men, saying, Whoever is fearful and trembling, let him turn back and depart from Mount Gilead. And 22,000 of the men returned, but 10,000 remained.

4And the Lord said to Gideon, The men are still too many; bring them down to the water, and I will test them for you there. And he of whom I say to you, This man shall go with you, shall go with you; and he of whom I say to you, This man shall not go with you, shall not go.

5So he brought the men down to the water, and the Lord said to Gideon, Everyone who laps up the water with his tongue as a dog laps it, you shall set by himself, likewise everyone who bows down on his knees to drink.

6And the number of those who lapped, putting their hand to their mouth, was 300 men, but all the rest of the people bowed down upon their knees to drink water.

7And the Lord said to Gideon, With the 300 men who lapped I will deliver you, and give the Midianites into your hand. Let all the others return every man to his home.

8So the people took provisions and their trumpets in their hands, and he sent all the rest of Israel every man to his home and retained those 300 men. And the host of Midian was below him in the valley.

9That same night the Lord said to Gideon, Arise, go down against their camp, for I have given it into your hand.

10But if you fear to go down, go with Purah your servant down to the camp

11And you shall hear what they say, and afterward your hands shall be strengthened to go down against the camp. Then he went down with Purah his servant to the outposts of the camp of the armed men.

12And the Midianites and the Amalekites and all the sons of the east lay along the valley like locusts for multitude; and their camels were without number, as the sand on the seashore for multitude.

13When Gideon arrived, behold, a man was telling a dream to his comrade. And he said, Behold, I dreamed a dream, and behold, a cake of barley bread tumbled into the camp of Midian and came to the tent and struck it so that it fell, and turned it upside down so that the tent lay flat.

14And his comrade replied, This is nothing else but the sword of Gideon son of Joash, a man of

Israel. Into his hand God has given Midian and all the host.

15When Gideon heard the telling of the dream and its interpretation, he worshiped and returned to the camp of Israel and said, Arise, for the Lord has given into your hand the host of Midian.

16And he divided the 300 men into three companies, and he put into the hands of all of them trumpets and empty pitchers, with torches inside the pitchers.

17And he said to them, Look at me, then do likewise. When I come to the edge of their camp, do as I do.

18When I blow the trumpet, I and all who are with me, then you blow the trumpets also on every side of all the camp and shout, For the Lord and for Gideon!

19So Gideon and the 100 men who were with him came to the outskirts of the camp at the beginning of the middle watch, when the guards had just been changed, and they blew the trumpets and smashed the pitchers that were in their hands.

20And the three companies blew the trumpets and shattered the pitchers, holding the torches in their left hands, and in their right hands the trumpets to blow [leaving no chance to use swords], and they cried, The sword for the Lord and Gideon!

21*They stood every man in his place round about the camp, and all the [Midianite] army ran--they cried out and fled.*

22*When [Gideon's men] blew the 300 trumpets, the Lord set every [Midianite's] sword against his comrade and against all the army, and the army fled as far as Beth-shittah toward Zererah, as far as the border of Abel-meholah by Tabbath.*

23*And the men of Israel were called together out of Naphtali and Asher and all Manasseh, and they pursued Midian.*

24*And Gideon sent messengers throughout all the hill country of Ephraim, saying, Come down against the Midianites and take all the intervening fords as far as Beth-barah and also the Jordan. So all the men of Ephraim were gathered together and took all the fords as far as Beth-barah and also the Jordan.*

25*And [the men of Ephraim] took the two princes of Midian, Oreb and Zeeb, and they slew Oreb at the rock of Oreb, and Zeeb they slew at the winepress of Zeeb, and pursued Midian; and they brought the heads of Oreb and Zeeb to Gideon beyond the Jordan.* (Judges 6:11-7:25 AMP)

Gideon was not unlike most men. He had greatness within him but he didn't know it. If he ever had known it, somewhere along the line of life, with all the problems, troubles, and trials, he forgot about the greatness. That's the way most of us are. Somewhere along the line we call life, we start dealing with the daily battles and forget to continue heading toward the finish line.

In this particular story, Gideon had a destiny that could be fulfilled. The Israelites had been under oppression of the Midianites. The country was in immediate trouble and Gideon was beating wheat in the winepress to hide it from the Midianites. God sent an angel of the Lord to Gideon. The angel appeared to him while he was working and said to him, *"The Lord is with you, you mighty man of [fearless] courage."*

Well, what a shocker! First, he was secretly working; trying to hide the wheat so he and his family would not starve and God sent an angel. This angel does not simply appear to him, but also brings him this crazy salutation! *"The Lord is with you, you mighty man of [fearless] courage."*

This should have been good news to Gideon. This should have been encouraging to his spirit but apparently it was not! Gideon answered right back to the angel of the Lord with these words, *"...sir, if the Lord is with us, why is all this befallen us?"*

Gideon said what many of us have said more than once! "Why?" "Why me, Lord?" "If the Lord is with me then why are all these bad things happening to me and my family? Where are You, Lord? What are You doing?"

Gideon didn't stop there. He proceeded to question the Lord even further. *"Where are You, Lord?" "Where are all Your wondrous works of which our fathers told us?"* (Paraphrased)

Even after these 'why' and 'where' questions had come forth from his mouth, Gideon didn't stop there. He said to the angel of the Lord, *"But now the Lord has forsaken us and given us into the hand of Midian."*

Wouldn't you think that these direct questions from Gideon followed by such an obvious statement of his abandoned feelings would have provoked some direct answers from the Lord to defend Himself as to 'why' and 'where'? But they didn't. In fact, the Lord did not respond at all to what Gideon said, but rather went more in line with the fact that He had not heard a word Gideon had said! The Lord's words back to Gideon were a direct command of something for Gideon to do. *"Go in this your might, and you shall save Israel from the hand of Midian. Have I not sent you?"*

Whoa there, God! First You come in here telling me that You are with me, that I am a mighty man of fearless courage, and now You tell me I gotta go and save Israel! Have You not heard one thing I have been saying? Have You not heard one of my questions? Am I supposed to go on ahead and not get one of my many questions answered? You expect me to 'Go' when I am stuck here in 'Why?'

Uh, yes, that is exactly right. Even when we get stuck in the 'who,' 'what,' 'when,' 'where,' 'how,' and 'why' questions of the flesh, which you might have noticed there are only six of these types of questions. Six is the number in Hebrew for 'flesh.' These are all our flesh questions! God is spirit and truth, not flesh. If we allow ourselves to get bogged down in flesh questions we may never be able to move forward and fulfill our destiny!

We can stop and set up camp by all our questions. We can dig our heels in and say that we are not leaving this spot until we get some answers to our questions. There is one thing about my God that I have learned. He is not obligated to answer any of my flesh questions. Nor does His divine will and purpose for my life change just because I get rebellious and stubborn.

In verse 15, we can see where Gideon goes on with another one of his questions when he asked, *"...how can I deliver Israel? Behold, my clan is the poorest in Manasseh, and I am the least in my father's house."*

Where we come from, who we come from, what we come through has no bearing on our destiny unless we give it a right to affect us. God stayed with the destiny He had set for Gideon. No matter how inadequate Gideon felt, no matter how Gideon rehearsed to God who he was not, God continued to push him to his destiny.

The greatest of all promises to break our self-consciousness, to null and void the lies of the enemy that would try and keep us from doing what God has created us to do was spoken by God in verse 16. *"The Lord said to him, "Surely I will be with you, and you shall smite the Midianites as one man."*

If only we could all grasp this truest of all true statements, "The Lord is with me."

This isn't the end of Gideon's questioning. Sadly, Gideon is so insecure about himself, his own ability, and his usefulness to the Lord that he continued on for quite some time testing the Lord through various fleeces. He wanted a word from the Lord and he got a word from the Lord. He wanted a sign from the Lord and he got a sign from the Lord. He wanted a few more signs, some outright weather-related miracles, not once but twice, and he got them all. Everything he asked God for, God accommodated Gideon. Finally, Gideon agreed to fulfill his destiny in God's plan. The story didn't end there. Actually it really just began. Once Gideon started obeying the plan, God started undoing everything Gideon thought about winning, and how to win against the enemy.

Everybody knows that 'might makes right.' Everybody knows that the biggest army always wins. Everybody knows that the largest organizations have the most effectiveness. Everybody knows that the largest churches do the most good, right?

Gideon had 32,000 in his army to go up against Midian. God told him that he had too many! God told him to proclaim in the ears of the men that whoever is fearful and trembling, let him turn back and depart from Mount Gilead. Well, wouldn't you know it? 22,000 of them went back! 22,000 were fearful and trembling and with one little suggestion to leave if they were afraid, off they went!

That left Gideon with 10,000 men. The Lord said to Gideon that there were still too many. God instructed Gideon to bring them down to the water, and He would test them there for him. That's a nice thought and a great promise. When God sends you on a mission, and people come to help you accomplish it, one of the hardest things is to truly know what is in another person's heart. What is their motive? Here we have a perfect example that God Himself will test them for us to prove who should be with us and who should not be.

God told Gideon that as He tested them, He would tell Gideon who should go with him and who should not go with him. Gideon brought the men down to the water, and the Lord said to Gideon in chapter seven, verse five, *"Everyone who laps up the water with his tongue as a dog laps it; you shall set by himself, likewise everyone who bows down on his knees to drink."*There were 300 men who lapped but all the rest of the people bowed down upon their knees to drink the water. The Lord told Gideon to take the 300 men who lapped the water and that would be his army. God told Gideon to send all the other men home! It's not like Gideon was this great man of faith. He didn't feel worthy at all to be there. Well at least he had a large army of 32,000 men! Wrong! God got his 32,000 men down to 300 warriors and that is what God used to subdue and conquer an entire army of the enemy!

> You may not see yourself as a man with greatness, but God has already put greatness within you!

Gideon could not see himself as a great man, but God knew what was within him. You may not see yourself as a man with greatness, but God has already put greatness within you! We all need to understand that even though we may have come through some heartbreaking experiences in life, that does not change the fact that greatness is within each one of us. We did not put it there. God put it there!

It took me figuring out that there is nothing within my own strength or power that can help me be who I am created to be. It is only when I recognized the greatest need in my life, the need for a father, not just any father, but God, my ultimate, always faithful, always true Father, that I could begin to get past all the inadequacies I felt, and look to the finisher of me, my Father God. He knows me, and He loves me anyway. He knows I am full of questions, and He still wants to use me. He knows what I cannot do. All He is asking of me is to know what He can do and then let Him do it, through me!

Remember it said in Judges that the Holy Spirit clothed Gideon with Himself. When we can figure out that we can't do it alone and we rely on God, He steps in and clothes us, surrounds us, and He provides what we need. When we go out we don't go in our own strength, or might, and we are no longer seen as just an individual but people see us shining in His glory, His might, and His strength. For that we are somebody to be reckoned with!

When I realized later in life and I mean later, it wasn't until Gabrielle was diagnosed with an inoperable brain tumor that I needed to rely on someone else, because I couldn't fix this. It was out of my power or ability. I couldn't even pay a doctor to fix it. So I truly had to rely on God, and I had a need, not personally but for my six-year-old little girl. You will find that you will do anything for your children. I did. I found out that when I asked one of our spiritual fathers for advice he said, "I can't make that decision for you." I thought that he was copping out on me. Later, I thought he was saying, "If I give you the wrong advice, you will blame me for the wrong outcome." But in reality, what he was saying and doing was very much like Eli talking with Samuel in I Samuel. I mentioned earlier how Samuel was hearing the voice of the Lord but because he had not been in relationship with God He didn't recognize the voice and thought it was Eli talking to him. After three times of Samuel running to Eli when he heard someone calling him, Eli knew it was God trying to speak directly to Samuel. Eli gave Samuel good instructions. Remember, he told him to go back and lie down and be still and wait. He told Samuel when you hear that voice again, this time respond, "It's me, Lord, Your servant, and I am listening." So, the priest, Eli was telling Samuel to expect God's voice, listen and answer when He calls. What can we take away from this? Get into position and expect to hear the voice of the Lord, and when you do, listen and answer!

My spiritual father was telling me the same thing. He was telling me to, "Go and listen to the voice of the Lord to speak to you. You already have a relationship with the Lord and now instead of not needing Him or relying on Him, submit yourself to Him and listen. It is God whom you need to hear from right now, not a man or woman."

So many times we think we hear God; we hear words and sounds, but we don't always listen. In the ancient Hebrew, [3]*hear* actually means to *hear with your ear, to understand with your mind, and to obey what you have heard and understood.* When we hear from God we must learn to act on the Word we have heard. We must learn to obey.

Many times we get our wants mixed up with our needs. God doesn't say He meets our wants. He meets our needs. Our daughter, Gabrielle, went home to be with the Lord on November 23, 1999. I wanted her healed so very badly and I needed her in my life. This is a very sticky area. Am I saying that God didn't heal her because I wanted her healed? Of course, not! That is not what I am saying. I am saying that God is a sovereign God and He did what He did, period. I don't have to understand to trust Him. I can live with the fact that she was healed ultimately as she entered heaven. Gabrielle is not in my past but she is in my future. She is not coming back to me, but I can go to her, in God's time.

After Gabrielle crossed over to heaven I needed my family restored. I felt so guilty too, as if I had in some way failed to provide enough covering to keep her here with us and to get her healed. What a lie of the devil that one is. As if God would actually rely on me instead of my relying on Him! How ridiculous and self-focused we can become in our egotistical, little, mirrored world of self!

I needed Cheryl to be healed. I needed our sons to be happy again. I needed God to be the head of our family as He designed it to be. **But He could not be the head of our family until He became the head of the head of the family!** Namely, me! That meant I had to let Him be God, a big God, big enough and equipped for all things. I was human and there were things I wasn't equipped to bear. The God of the universe cares enough about me and my family to hear my prayers and to meet our needs! It took me recognizing and realizing that I could not bear the burden or guilt or whatever of having our daughter pass away. My shoulders were not broad enough, my arms were not large enough, nor was my will great enough to bring restoration to my family.

When I left it in His hands I realized that He is a big God. Even when I was mad at Him because Gabrielle passed, I would wake up and still have a relationship with Him. He is our heavenly Father and He knows that the need for someone or something in my life was being fulfilled because I ultimately had no other options but to trust Him. I caution you though – being mad or upset with God is alright just like being mad at our sons or fathers, when we wake up we are still in relationship because it's surface emotion. But when we allow anger to set in, it becomes something deep-rooted. I never got angry with God because I had worked so hard at establishing a relationship with Him, I didn't want anything to ruin that. Anger is deep-rooted. Don't let anger get inside of you and take root. Get upset, mad, unhappy – okay, but anger, in my opinion, is a whole different story. It deals with the heart, and no one needs that much strain on their heart.

It was not just a change in my mind, but a change of my heart!

I pray you never have to get to the same place that I did. I pray that you learn to trust Him, to rely on Him to be God in your life, personally as the need-meeter for your life!

Chapter Eight

Father's Day

All my life I had 'head knowledge' of God. I knew God. I knew who He was, what His names were, how to get in touch with Him when I needed Him. But I also knew there had to be more, and there was. My greatest need was not a replacement dad. My greatest need was a personal relationship with the greatest of all Fathers, the Father who made me just like I am!

> My greatest need was a personal relationship with the greatest of all Fathers...

I thought that once I had children and I became a father that the void in my life for this father/son relationship would be fulfilled, but I was wrong. I even thought that because we had two sons that God was somehow making up double for the loss of my father. But even my children could not fill the empty void within my soul.

We all want our children to have it better than we did. So I determined that I could have the father/son relationship that I so longed for through my being the father. I don't believe I could have ever truly become the kind of father God intended for me to be to our children, until I accepted Him as my true Father God. Once I learned how to accept His unconditional love and forgiveness, I have learned how to love and forgive my own children as they grow and learn how to be God's men.

Now every birthday and Father's Day my greatest treasures are the gifts from our sons. It's not the shirts and ties, or the funny way they wrap things, but each birthday and Father's Day both Harry and Roman write me a letter and give me a card. These cards are precious to me, but these hand-written scribbled writings are the dearest and most valuable possessions of this father's life. They express their love for me in words which took them time to think about and write down. These letters mean so much to me because first, they come from my children. Second, they took time to write them. Third, they spoke from their hearts. And the last thing, and maybe it is a bit selfish on my part, but these letters validate to me that the desire to have a father/son relationship with my children has paid off and I have accomplished what I set out to do for my children. Yes, it's still hard on Father's Day because there are only two letters instead of three. But **I can't focus on what I don't have or I will lose what I do have**, as Cheryl has said many times.

Usually, they put some funny story, or silly something, or ridiculous event we shared together that year. Without a doubt those letters which I keep in a special place are the dearest to me. They are so special that I carry two in my Bible at all times.

When I have a down day, I take out my letters and read them. One by one they lift my spirit, and remind me once again that my greatest need, the deepest longing of my heart is fulfilled first toward my heavenly Father, who is God and Lord to me, then toward my wonderful children, whose very lives shout restoration to my soul each and every day.

I realize that if these letters of love expressed in words meant so much to me how much more it would mean to my heavenly Father if I were to have that kind of relationship with Him. Knowing the love of our children has helped me learn how valuable and precious my Father/son relationship is with my eternal Father. He longs for me far more than I could ever long for Him. He loves me far more than I could ever love Him. He is love! I am learning to ask my Father to teach me how to love Him.

People have said to me that I must be a great father because we have great children. I used to answer them like, "No, I think we have great children in spite of anything I, as a father, could ever do." A part of that might be true, but I have come to realize that in my attempt to be humble, or contrite, or simply polite I may have missed the point.

Most of the time great children do not just happen. They are a product of great fathers and mothers and much time spent parenting, learning, and growing together as a family. When I think of my own journey in life, I realize that as a son of God, I did not become a great son in spite of my Father God, but because of Him. We are all great children, and greatness is within us, but it is not in spite of what our heavenly Father has done for us. It is *because* of what our heavenly Father has done for us!

Yes, now I accept that my wife and I have great children because of a great Father God to us all, who teaches us in all truth, who guides us in all wisdom, who loves us beyond anything we can imagine. For those things we have done right as parents, we humbly say, "Thank You, Lord." For those things we have done wrong as parents, we ask God to forgive us, and help us make it right. We ultimately do the best we know how, and then we have to trust God with our children and the end result of their lives. We must trust that as He drew us to Himself, He will also draw our children. What's our part in all this? Teach our children to listen to God, to obey His voice, to act quickly to His leading. We teach, they learn, God does the rest. He is, after all, the ultimate Father.

You know, Father's Day to me isn't just to be celebrated once a year. Neither should you communicate with your Father once a year just when you want something. If my sons just talked to me once a year or when they wanted something I probably would say they don't really love me or want to spend time with me, and I would probably be right too! Would we have a real relationship if they just wanted me to be the bank, or the provider, the problem-solver, the fixer, or the doctor? It's daily time spent with them that gives them the things to put down in writing to me on a Father's Day card. If you are having a tough time writing down on the next journal page your thoughts towards your heavenly Father, I wonder if you are spending much time with Him on a daily basis? It's said if you live to be 70 years old and give God five minutes in the morning, and five minutes in the evening, and go to church once a week that we would be giving God only five months of our cntire lives! Yet we want to rule and reign with Him for eternity and have Him provide us with a mansion on streets of gold in heaven!

So many times our sons come into our room at night and just sit at the foot of our bed and talk about the day. They often ask how our day has gone. We almost have to make them leave our room so we can go to sleep. That kind of relationship didn't happen overnight. It started with us talking to them and then listening to them, too. Being a good listener as a father is much better than being a good talker. That's why I think **God is always listening to us** and when He speaks to us it is so impactful to our lives. When He talks it's rich with wisdom, fruitful, exciting, and encouraging! Even if it is only one word, or one phrase, a short conversation with God is like well... remember **a little gold is still gold**!

Take a little time to write your heavenly Father a letter. Tell Him how much you love Him, how much you appreciate what He has done for you in your life. You might be surprised what this will do for you! Be honest, speak from your heart. He knows your heart already, so no need to hide anything.

You might be saying that you don't know where to start. Here's one! Let's see if I can prime your pump!

Thank You, Lord, for giving me life, for allowing me to be in Your family.

Remember, we don't just have a great father, we have the greatest Father, our heavenly Father. Greatness is within you. You come from very good stock, royalty, to be exact. You are a king's kid.

Chapter Nine

Responsibility of a True Father

When my wife and I teach about having a good marriage, we often refer to the differences between men and women. We have come to learn that it is our very differences that we need to learn to celebrate, because if we are just alike, then one of us is unnecessary! We complete the picture of a whole image by taking each side, the right and the left, the up and the down. Husbands and wives are generally polar opposites! But in those opposites we maintain the balance of life, the balance of relationship, the balance in family, and the balance in the universe!

We have shared this for many years and we have found that sometimes men will come up and say, "Hey, I am more like your wife than you!" And then other times women will come up to us and say, "I have many more personality traits of your husband than of you, Cheryl." What we have discovered is even though there are a few times when the roles are reversed; it is obvious that people tend to marry the opposite of who they are. While we are quick to admit these are not male/female traits as much as they are the traits that the Lord desires and needs to be in each relationship for balance, we will list them the way we portray them in our individual roles in our marriage. Remember to celebrate your differences, not tolerate or despise them! It's cute; it's funny so enjoy it! Have fun with it. Lighten up. Life is too short to be so uptight over things you cannot change!

►Men are logical. Women are illogical.

►Men are physical. Women are emotional.

►Men want the headlines. Women want the details.

►Men are file cabinets. Women are computers.

►Men are life-givers. Women are life-receivers.

►Men give the seed. Women give the harvest.

►Men are turned on by sight. Women are turned on by touch.

►Men want sex. Women want love.

►Men are fixers. Women are menders.

►Men deal with immediate problems. Women deal with potential problems.

►Men want the toilet seat up. Women want the toilet seat down.

►Men want sex. Women want to cuddle.

►Men want sex. Women want intimacy.

►Men deal in 'thoughts.' Women deal in 'feelings.'

►Oh, I almost forgot! Did I mention that ...

MEN WANT SEX!!!!!!

There's no really nice way to get around this very important fact. Men want sex. Men need sex. But as fathers, we must not only teach responsibility but live responsibly in the face of Almighty God and as examples to our children, especially our sons!

As men, we need to be extremely careful to not use manipulation to get what we want and need. Let's take a moment and talk about the responsibility of sex and love. There is a huge responsibility that comes with the act of making love or the physical function of sex. Rearing two sons, we must have 'the talk' with them. When is the right time? That answer you must determine on your own. It's a unique decision, based upon knowing your children through relationship.

Here's what happened to me and how I knew it was time to have at least a portion of the talk. Cheryl had been telling me that the boys had asked her a lot of questions. At that time in our lives, I was working many hours a day, so she spent a good deal of the time with them during the week. On the weekends she would fly to preach somewhere and I would have the boys with me.

I guess the boys had been asking what Cheryl considered to be father/son questions not mother/son questions and she told me I should have a discussion with them. So we were riding in the car; I was driving, Roman in the front seat, and Harry III sitting in the back seat. I was not quite sure how to broach the subject so I just kind of threw it out there to see which one bit first.

I said, "Well, boys, tell me what you know about sex." Now Harry III has been a reader all his life. He studies, has vast knowledge of all kinds of things, not from experience but from his mind in the adventures of books. So with that baited question came the intellectual brain to give me his version. Harry III began by going through the entire science version of the birds and the bees. We had flowers, and the stamen, the pollen, and the bees. We had much fruitfulness flowing out of his mouth to the point it was hard for me to suppress a huge smile. As I drove listening intently, I noticed Roman wiggling and squirming all over the front seat. He was definitely agitated about something!

Once Harry III finally wound down his rendition of the science and history channel, Roman blurted out, "Aw, Harry (pronounced Hawwy), you're getting it all wrong!" Now I could tell that Roman was convinced that at four years old (yes, I said four years old!) he knew much more about this subject than his much older and wiser brother, all of seven by now!

I gave Roman a sideways glance and said, "Ok, Roman, tell me what you know."

Roman took in a deep breath and with all the confidence a four-year-old could muster on the subject of sex he proclaimed, "Kissing is the first step to intercourse!"

Well, I about wrecked the car! I could hardly believe my ears! What in this world had those children at the church preschool been teaching my innocent child! I looked straight ahead as the silence filled the car like fog filled the London streets in a Sherlock Holmes movie! I had to get my composure before I could make a comment.

I finally let out my breath and said, "Really, Roman. So just where did you learn that?"

Without hesitation or fear Roman almost shouted, "Mama says, 'Kissing is the first step to intercourse.'" Now I did smile as I said, "Oh, so Mama says that, huh?"

Roman, as sweet as pie, said, "Yes, Daddy, that's right!"

I just could not think of one thing to say after that bold statement. So I drove, with both my hands gripping the steering wheel in front of me, and not taking my eyes off the road as these two most worldly and knowledgeable young men of four and seven sat absolutely stoically in the car with their dumbfounded dad. In their minds, all was right with the world.

They had no idea that I was laughing hysterically inside, slapping my leg with belly laughter, but not a sign of it on my face! So after many moments of silence as we rode through the roads of the life of two young men, I said, "Well, do you have any questions?"

Of course, I was hoping they were completely satisfied and had absolutely not a clue as to any questions they might need answers to. But I was not to be blessed that day. I noticed to my right, out of the corner of my eye, Roman had his hand raised with a definite question.

I braced myself for what might possibly come out of his mouth next as he asked, "Yes, Daddy, I have one question."

I politely said, "Well, sure, son. What's your question."

He looked at me with the wide-eyed innocence that engulfed his mind and heart and said, "What's intercourse?"

Well, I was up for just about anything, but answering a four year old on that particular subject I had no idea where to begin! So without hesitation or any hint of fear in my voice I answered back to him, "Ask your mother." He nodded his little head in complete satisfaction. And with that, it was over!

As the boys got bigger and their questions needed more than a mother's touch, they needed to be dealt with father to sons. As they entered their teenage years, the time was apparent they needed 'the talk' from their dad. I prayed and sought the Lord on what to say, and what not to say.

I felt that giving instructions was not going to satisfy and explain what I felt the Lord wants these young men to know in this generation. It wasn't actually the talk about staying pure, or abstaining from sex; but the first and most important talk we had was about respect of a woman. When a young man is taught to respect a young lady, it helps him see clearly God's plan for relationships. It helps him distinguish and see the difference between the act of sex and the love between a man and a woman. Sex is set up by God. It's a supernatural event in the life of two people becoming one. It's covenant; it is a flesh covenant, and it's real. It is a bond, a binding together by choice of the mind, will, and emotions, then completed by the physical act of intimacy during sex.

Young men and women will never understand the importance of the covenant of sex until they understand the responsibility of respect.

Harry was getting older and our six-foot tall son was wanting to be treated like a man. He wanted adult respect and responsibilities. On one particular occasion his mama told him to do something, and he disrespected her and said that he didn't have to do it. I think he said something like, "Cheryl, I don't want to, and I don't have to." A loud discussion occurred (An argument most would call it! Cheryl calls it a discussion with attitude!).

I heard what was going on, so I stepped in and took Harry aside and said, "You want to be treated like a man?" He said, "Yes." I asked again, "You think you are a man?" He quickly answered, "Yes." I said, "Okay. I'm going to deal with you like any other man I know." He said, "Okay." I said, "I want you to know THAT BEFORE SHE WAS YOUR MAMA SHE WAS MY WIFE. After you were born she became your mama. But she is still my wife, first and foremost. And now that you are grown, and you say you want to be treated like an equal man. Even though she is still your mama, I want you to know that she is my wife. And I am not going to let you or any other man talk to my wife like that. So man to man, if you ever treat my wife like that again, you and I are going to settle this man to man! You understand?"

His eyes got wide and I am quite certain he got the picture and had no doubt what I meant. He calmly said, "Yes, Dad." And went into the other room and found his mama. He took her in his arms and turned her to him face to face and said, "Mom, I'm sorry."

Children don't do what you tell them to do. They do what you do.

So the first step to train up your sons or 'have the talk with them' is to teach them to respect the first woman in their lives, their mom. And that can only be done when you respect your wife. We have said this for years. **Children don't do what you tell them to do. They do what you do.**

Understanding the true respect of a woman will lead them to want to love a woman and not just want to perform the physical act of sex with a woman.

Maybe you are thinking that I am out of my mind in this, but I think not. I can tell you that our sons respect and love their mom and if I get off track they come in and say, "Dad, you were wrong and you need to go apologize to Mom." Instead of me saying, "You don't know what you are talking about," I realize they do know what they are talking about because I taught them!

The women in our lives have been entrusted to us, just as our children have been entrusted into our care. When we misuse them in any way, we will have to answer to our Father God. In my entire life I have never been more 'pulled up short' than when the Lord God called upon me to treat His daughter with care and tenderness. It was as if I was going on my very first date and the dad was standing at the door to meet me while his daughter continued to get ready for our date. When God, the ultimate Father of us all, stared me down, melted my heart and spoke into the very core of my being with these words. **"Your greatest responsibility is to take care of My daughter."** All of a sudden, I had the realization that God Almighty not only is my Father, but He is also my Father-in-law! He will personally hold me responsible for the way I treat

His daughter! It is a sobering thought, one which I have continued to consider after decades of marriage. I want to make my heavenly Father proud of me, but I also want to show Him that I am trustworthy and can take care of His daughter as well!

God Almighty not only is my Father... He is also my Father-in-law!

Remember, our responsibility as husbands is to take care of our heavenly Father's earthly daughter. When you look at your wife that way, I believe you will see her differently. That's where I think the Bible says dress her in dazzling white apparel (Ephesians 5:27 MSG) because she is God's daughter on loan to you so take care of her. She is not a house wife, she is your wife, she is not a home maker, she makes the home, she is not your servant she is your help mate, and all of us men need help. Because one day you will be standing before Him and He will know how you treated His daughter.

In studying about a man and a woman, I remember the scripture in I Corinthians 13:11 that says when I became a man I put away childish things.

"When I was a child, I spoke as a child, I understood as a child, I thought as a child; but when I became a man, I put away childish things."

Taking that in complete context and understanding takes breaking it down for me. It would have been easier for God to have said that at a certain age we would all mature into adults and become men. I know that certain cultures say that at a certain age their males become recognized as men. But we all know that it is not possible to simply assign an age to when a person develops mentally, emotionally, physically, and spiritually to become a man. It is in the putting away of childish things, that in God's eyes, we are recognized as truly being processed into manhood.

In my understanding, it breaks down like this. There is an appointed time in a man's life, set forth by the design of God, for that boy to become a man. But let's not focus on an age, as we all know it has very little if anything to do with an actual age. I know many men who still act like little boys and I know little boys who actually act like men.

On that Saturday morning when I was ten years old and my father was in the hospital dying with leukemia, he told me three things. The first was to never trust anyone. At least that is what I heard him say. Whether that is what he actually said or not, I cannot know on this earth. As I have analyzed what his words actually were I think he was saying there is no one else in the world you should trust more than your family. But that is not what I heard.

The second thing he said was for me to never be a sucker for anyone. Well, there goes the problem with trust. My earthly father told me never to trust anyone. What did I hear? I heard that if I could not trust my earthly father to not die and leave me here on the earth, how could I trust my heavenly Father to be here for me when I needed Him? I now know that is not what my earthly father actually said, but like I said before, it was what I heard. If my earthly father abandoned me and took away my father/son relationship through death then how could I trust to have a heavenly Father/son relationship? My little mind went straight to abandonment/rejection thinking mode from that time on in my life.

After much prayer and thought about these words spoken over me as a little boy, I now think my dad was telling me to always ask questions and question the heart, the motive of the heart of those around me, to be cautious in life and to not fall for the wolves in sheep's clothing. I truly believe he was trying, in a few lines of a conversation, to teach me about life because he knew his time with his son was short. But we all know that life can't be learned in a few lines, or a few conversations, or a few days, weeks, months or even years. Life is learned over a lifetime and with deep commitments of relationships surrounding us in every direction.

The last thing my father told me was that I was, at that very moment, a man – and that men don't cry. And he added, "Don't cry at my funeral." He didn't just say I was a man, but he told me that I was the man of the house from that day forth and I was to take care of my mom. He was still alive, talking to me! I was ten years old! I had no idea that he was actually telling me that he was about to die and for me to get ready for his funeral. He was telling me that people, family, and friends would put undue pressure on me as a boy to stand up and be a man! I continually heard him say, "Men don't cry."

It became instantly clear to me in the middle of the night when my mother came home from the hospital with my grandfather as they woke me up and told me my father was gone, and had me get my sisters. They then told them of our father's passing. My sisters went back to bed but my mother had me go and take down all the pictures of my father in the entire house and put them in the closet. I didn't understand at that time but now I know that it was going to be too hard on my mother to look at those pictures on a daily basis. I know this now because when our daughter passed to heaven, I took all her pictures down. It was simply too hard to look at her face. As a side note, I want you to know and be encouraged I believe that if you have a loved one that has passed before you to heaven that those feelings of overwhelming grief will eventually lessen and you will be able to once again look at those pictures without the heart-wrenching pain of before.

After a year or so passed when we were left without our Gabrielle, Cheryl was after me to take a family photo. In my mind, I was never going to take another family photo because the family was not all present to be in the picture. I know now how illogical that was. I was completely focused on who we did not have, and totally 'missing' the two sons we did have with us on the earth. As usual, Cheryl eventually won out. She hired the photographer to come to the house since I was not going to go anywhere to get the pictures taken. I came home from work one day and the photographer was setting up. The amazing thing is before this day, the very night before, I had felt the Lord impress upon me that it was time to go and get Gabrielle's last portrait and hang it in our formal living room on the mantle. I put it up and never said a word to anyone else in the house. I simply obeyed the Lord in this.

When I arrived home on the following day, here was the photographer setting up for the family portrait in the living room. I can't say that I was easy to work with on this, or even nice to my family or the photographer but under orders of my precious wife, I sat! I was literally under protest. This was too difficult for me. I just could not imagine looking at pictures of our family of four and not five anymore.

I had already had a glimpse into what this was going to look like. Because soon after Gabrielle passed, we took the boys to Universal Studios to get them out of the house and try and change the environment. We tried to let them be little boys again without constant doctors, diagnoses, blood tests, and medicine all around them. When we went in to the theme park there was a person who stepped up who worked for the studio and took our picture. They then gave us a receipt and said that at the end of the day on our way out to go to this particular spot and we could purchase our picture. Well at the end of the day we did as they had instructed and they showed us the photo. It had the characters for the theme park in the picture. Roman, Harry, Mama, and me, but no Gabrielle.

I put the photo down and walked out leaving without saying a word. Roman said, "Dad, where's the picture?" I told him that it cost too much, but really I just couldn't bear to see Gabrielle missing from our family picture!

After we had our photo shoot in our home, we received the proofs back and I didn't want to even take a look at them. I was being so stubborn about it and finally Cheryl insisted that I look at them. To my amazement there was our family of five staring right back at me. In the picture there was Cheryl, our sons, Harry III, Roman, and me, but over our shoulder was the beautiful face of our daughter, Gabrielle, through her latest portrait on the mantle. She was not left out at all! The Lord spoke to my heart and said that **Gabrielle will always be in the family picture.**

Of course, she will be in our family forever because although she is not with us in the flesh, she is with us in spirit and lives in our hearts and memories. Even more than that, **Gabrielle is not in our past but she is in our future.** She is alive and well and living in the eternal realm of heaven. This is very important to me as her father. I know that she is safe and sound, with no possibility of ever being hurt or wounded again. Our little girl is in her heavenly Father's arms. I don't necessarily like it, but it is the way that it is, and looking at the whole picture for all of eternity, I can go on and live my

Gabrielle is not in our past but she is in our future.

life while I am still here on earth. But don't get me wrong or misunderstand what I am saying. I didn't get here in my thinking overnight, and I still don't like it. It's just the way it is. I finally accept it as truth, and all truth will set us free if we let it!

Be encouraged! If you have a loved one who has gone home before you, they might not be here in the flesh, but they will never leave your heart. Heaven is a real place, not a figment of our imagination. Heaven is a destination where our eternal Father lives. He is building a house for us to live with Him for eternity.

How do you know when it's time to put the pictures back up or that you are being restored from grief and mourning? Well, for everyone the time is different. But a good clue is that we find ourselves talking about Gabrielle and the hilarious, clever, adorable things she would say or do. Now instead of those stories causing us to cry or hurt, we are laughing and enjoying our memories of her time with us. We had her on this earth for six years. Our sorrows have been turned into joy. We know we are on the other side of grief now.

That does not mean that we don't have our moments, even our days when we have to fight to keep our joy, and peace. Even last Christmas, after more than ten years of separation, we tried to watch a video of the family in an early year of our family around the Christmas tree. All the children were in it! And as sweet and happy as the children all were, and as fun as it was to see the boys as little men, the pain of watching Gabrielle was just too hard to bear. There may be a day we can, but not yet. It was just too much. But we tried and maybe someday we will get all the way through that video too!

I don't focus on the fact that we had to say goodbye to her, but I focus on the promise that one day, I'll be able to say hello to her again!

Now back to the night my earthly father died. My mother did not sleep in her bed that night. She went to the living room and asked me to sit on the sofa and she laid her head in my lap and went to sleep, or at least rested, until morning. I would be experiencing things and situations that most ten year-old boys would never have to experience. I was going to be dealing with things I should not have to deal with as a child. I won't say that it was unbearable because I had a good childhood. I played baseball, basketball, and football, and I enjoyed my time, I had a closeness with my mother that I don't think I would have had if this had not happened to my father. I would spend Friday nights playing Scrabble with her and cooking with her, spending more time with her than most boys would spend with their mothers. To this day I have a great bond with my mother that I am fairly certain began in those days following my dad's death. Of course, my bond with my mother could be that she spent 36 hours in labor trying to give me life and almost lost hers for me. Putting this book together, I see so plainly how my mom deserves so much credit for the outcome of my life. Between my heavenly Father, and my earthly mother, there was much to do for me! But this is all scriptural, as in Psalm 68:5, *"A father of the fatherless, a defender of widows, is God in His holy habitation."*

> I see so plainly how my mom deserves so much credit for the outcome of my life.

My mother was a small, dainty woman but she was the strength of the family. My father, believing he was going to die, told my mother that he did not want a grave stone. She asked him what he was talking about and he said, "I am a marine and the marines will provide me with a grave marker and that is what I want, so make sure that happens." And it did. As I mentioned earlier, it says on his grave marker: MARINE, SON, HUSBAND, FATHER. She took care of it all, she even was the one that taught me to kick a football. I can still see her now with her red Keds tennis shoes kicking the football and breaking the blood vessels in her foot. When I said, "Now I'll never learn to kick a football," her reply was, "Oh yes you will, but tomorrow I will wear socks." She was small and dainty but she was determined to see her family through.

Becoming a man isn't attached to an age. Many times it is attributed to the situations and circumstances surrounding a boy's life. As I put away childish things, I discovered those are more emotional and mental than actually physical things. It's not when a child decides to put away his toys, as to this day I enjoy playing basketball with our sons. I enjoy playing video games with them and watching sports with them. It's about putting away thoughts and things in our lives that are not productive to our future lives as adults.

It's easier to blame someone else today, than to take responsibility.

It's maturing in the Lord that makes us adults. So many times we say we want God to speak to us. We want God to speak in an audible voice. But now I realize that as we spiritually mature, **He does speak to us and that communication is**

called 'discernment.' We don't need God to speak to our flesh, for our flesh ears to hear. We don't need someone audibly telling us what to do, but because we have grown close to Him and are in relationship with Him, and know and keep His commandments (all), He trusts us as mature Christians to discern right and wrong, good and evil, even what's hidden or masked. By trusting Him and hearing him through discernment, we will be able to see these things.

It is about prioritizing our lives with the things at the top that stand for responsibility. Responsibility is a huge void in the lives of men today. It is much easier to blame someone or something or some event that did or did not happen. But when it all comes down to it, it's like this. If someone wrongs you and you want to strike back at them, will you respond as an adult or react like a spoiled child? Will you act like a man or a boy? Our natural reaction is to hold on to hurt, and wear it like a badge of honor but the truth is, the only person who looks bad in those instances is the one who won't let it go. And truly the only person these types of emotional responses hurt is the one who is holding the hurt, the resentment, the bitterness. My wife says that **bitterness and unforgiveness is like drinking poison and expecting the other person to die.** The only person who is negatively affected for life is the one who won't forgive and turn it all loose. We can't control what others say or do, but we can control our responses to them.

Taking responsibility for something isn't always easy, and being a responsible father takes a lot more than I ever expected. Some men are just created to be more responsible in all ways. For others, it's a process. Don't give up. Stay faithful, God will reward you.

Harry & Mom (Patricia)

Chapter Ten

Responsibility:

But I Don't Want to be the Dad Today!

The responsibility of a father isn't always the fun part of parenting. In fact, it is nothing like I wanted it to be. It is not what commercials and TV shows make it look like, where we get to do all the barbequing and playing baseball with our kids, going to dance recitals, and watching our little girls be the cheerleader or the lead in the school play. No, our responsibility as the strong leader in the house is truly being father, taking our rightful position and not deferring all the tough decisions to our wives.

> Be the strong leader in your home that your family, your children and your wife need and desire.

Disciplining the children is not merely mom's responsibility. It is not in our best interest as a father, nor in our children's future best interest to always be passing the buck by saying, "Go ask your mother." When we show this type of weak behavior we already know the answer to the question. We just don't want to be the bad guy and have to say no to the cute little faces looking back at us. Talk about weak! Don't be weak!!! Be strong. **Be the strong leader in your home that your family,**

your children and your wife need and desire. Take responsibility. Become the man capable of leading your family and making hard decisions. Look at the example given to us – a tough decision was made by our Father God, when He sent His Son, Jesus Christ to the cross! No stronger decision has ever been made to show the benefit of strong leadership in the role as father as this one decision made by the ultimate of all ultimate Fathers.

Remember when Jesus was in the garden praying before the men came to get Him and lead Him away to be crucified? Remember how the Bible says that He was so stressed over His next move, His next obedience to His Father, that He was literally sweating blood? (Luke 22:43-44) That's a stress that we can hardly fathom, much less identify in our own lives. Jesus finally came to the decision of surrender when He simply prayed, *"Not My will, but Yours be done."* That settled it for all of eternity. That settled it for you, and me, and Himself, and everyone involved. That settled it for the enemy, the devil, who was stupid enough to think that he could actually kill the King of kings! That one decision settled deliverance, and redemption for all mankind who will receive forgiveness.

God's toughest decision, in my opinion, was to sacrifice His only Son for a people who had already rejected Him for centuries. God can see further down the road than we can though. And even though all the world will not receive Jesus Christ as Savior, and Redeemer, for the few who will, He still died once and for all, for us.

Strong dads mean strong homes!

[3]'**Abba**' comes from the **first two symbols** in the **ancient Hebrew language**. When I think of God's kind of true daddy, he is plan A and also plan B! The first letter of the Hebrew alphabet means **'strong,'** the second means **'house/home.'** So when we have dads in the home, we have a strong home! It's quite simple to see that God's perfect plan for godly homes, marriages, families, children and the training of the next generation starts and stops with fathers. **Strong dads mean strong homes!**

In the movie, "The Passion of the Christ," there is a scene in which Mary, the mother of Jesus, is portrayed after Jesus has been beaten and whipped. His blood is all over the ground and she is on her hands and knees collecting all the blood in linens. She could have never sent her Son, Jesus to the cross. No matter how much she would want to obey God, I don't believe she could have sent Him on her own to be crucified. But God, the Father of all, chose to send Jesus Christ, His only Son to pay the price and redeem back all of mankind with His blood. It took the strength of the Father to do this.

We, as humanity, would like to blame the Jews or the Romans, or Pilate for sending Jesus to the cross, but ultimately they were only players in the scene set up by God Himself. He sent His Son to die for us. God sent His Son to suffer, and be humiliated, beaten, and whipped, bruised, and ultimately crucified on a cross, the most horrific of all deaths. Jesus paid that price for us. No human made that call. God, the Father set it all up, and Jesus, the Son submitted to the plan. There is no one to blame. We have only God to thank and be grateful for this amazing gift of LOVE.

RESPONSIBILITY. What a powerful word for fathers. When I think of responsibility I remember an incident that happened when we lived in the Midwest. We had a two story house and the children were still small. They were always leaving one of the doors open. This particular time, the kids had left the front door open and it was summer time. As I walked by, I saw something out the corner of my eye. Before I could react, I knew it was a snake! It came in the open door and was going up the steps to one of the children's bedrooms! I followed it up the stairs as fast as I could. Those things are quick! I cornered it in the bedroom behind the dresser. I started yelling for Cheryl to come help me get this snake out of the house but she was nowhere to be found!

Now you have to understand, Cheryl grew up in the country (in the South, no less!) and snakes were in the grass, in the garden and all around there. I, on the other hand, grew up in the city, in Michigan, and snakes were not a part of my growing up years! I hate snakes! I don't even look at pictures of snakes or watch shows on television with snakes in them. When a snake is in a movie, I close my eyes! I don't like anything to do with snakes so to have one in my house was way beyond my comfort zone.

Roman came running when he heard me yelling and said, "What is it, Daddy?" I turned to him and said, "Roman, go to the garage and get me something to kill this snake!" I kept my eye on it so as not to lose it. It was wedged behind the dresser. I was staring at it and it was staring back at me, sticking its little tongue out. About that time, Roman came running back in the room and he handed me a pair of work gloves and needle-nosed pliers! I exclaimed to him, "Son! I said *kill* the snake, not *catch* the snake!" I tried to reach in with the pliers, but I just couldn't do it. About that time,

Harry came in the room and I said to both of them, "I just can't do it." Harry, with all of his mother wrapped up in his very being, exclaimed to me, "Dad! You can do all things though Christ who strengthens you!"

I sighed. I knew I had to do it. I had to get the snake. I reached in, and as I grabbed its head with the pliers, it wrapped itself around my arm. All the way down the hallway and the stairs I was yelling the same phrase over and over, "Why do I have to be the father? Why do I have to be the dad? Why me, Lord?"

I want you to know that this happened a second time later on, but I got smart! I called a friend of mine and asked would he please come over and help me with something. I told him I couldn't do this 'task' by myself, etc. Once he arrived at the house, I told him about the snake! Thank God for my friend. He was not afraid of the snake and he helped me get it out of the house! I had matured and learned that I don't have to do everything by myself! Some things are better shared with a friend!

The snake incidents were nerve-wracking at the time, but funny now. Just memories of days gone by and the life and times of a father. But there was another time in my fathering days, which by the way, are never over as long as our children are on the earth, that was devastating. Our children were young – Harry III was twelve years old, Roman was eight years old, and Gabrielle was five years old. We were blind-sided by the most horrible news possible. Our youngest child and only daughter, Gabrielle, was diagnosed with an inoperable brain tumor. We were faced with the decision of what treatment to choose. We really had no good choices. We had been told that no matter what we chose, nothing was going to cure her. We were told that no one had ever survived this type of brain tumor and no surgery was possible. We had heard nothing but bad news. Our only option that seemed at all valid was a type of experimental treatment that was extremely expensive and still did not give us much hope.

We were trying to apply God's Word by prayer with everything God put on this earth as well. Any medicine that could have offered any hope was more than we had been given. We had so many questions and hardly any answers. There were good doctors, and good hospitals but none of them could help us. We had decisions to make – huge, life-altering decisions, and I was the father! What do I do? What is the best option? Do we even have any options? How do we pay for this? These questions were coming like waves on the ocean in my mind.

What do I do? The expensive medicine which I know is going to put a financial hardship on our entire family is an option! This is our daughter's life we are talking about here, so money, no matter how much it is, should not be a consideration! No matter how much it costs, I would have to find a way to pay for it. She would have to have an open port in her chest and have this experimental medicine flowing through her little body 24 hours a day, 7 days a week. This was a huge decision! Do we just extend her life by radiation and chemotherapy even though they have already told us it would not cure her? If we do this treatment she will be deaf for sure, and very likely blind, they say. That's no option at all since the doctors have already told us this will only extend her life for a few more months and with what quality of life? We were told that no matter what we chose to do, even that which was 'recommended,' regardless, even if the tumor would shrink or even disappear, it would grow right back!

I remember being in our motor home with our children, all three of them were having pizza for dinner. We were in the city where the experimental treatment was to begin the very next day. The children wanted pizza. We got them pizza. We were parked behind a shopping center, next to two big trash dumpsters. The children were eating, and laughing, and having a good time and I walked out of the motor home for a moment to pray and collect my thoughts. I was asking God for direction, to guide me in my decision, but I got nothing in return from heaven. Not a sound, not one word did I hear from the throne room of God. I thought to myself that if only my father were alive he could help me with this decision. But he wasn't here and I found myself alone with a decision that was so important that it was going to affect something more important to me than myself. This decision was beyond me. It would have been easier to make the decision had it only affected me, but this decision affected me, my wife, our young sons, and our only little girl. Yes, this decision was way beyond my comfort zone of responsibility. I could not bear the thought of making the wrong decision concerning our daughter's life.

When I was to the point where I just could not even think clearly, I got a phone call from a friend. He was an older gentleman; he was a father and a grandfather too. Maybe he could help me make this decision. I took the opportunity to ask him what he would do in my situation. I waited for a fatherly answer to help me. But he said that he could not make that decision for me, because if he did and it turned out to be the wrong decision then I would have someone else to blame. He said, "I'm sorry but you are going to have to make this one on your own. Besides, you already know what to do.”

A best friend is someone you grow up with. A true friend is someone who helps you grow up!

I hung up and felt a big, hearty, sarcastic, “Thanks a lot,” coming up in my mind. I wanted to say, “And you call yourself my friend?” but now I realize that he said what a true friend should always do and say. **A best friend wants to tell you what you want to hear**; a best friend has such empathy and sympathy for us that many times they just want to make us feel better. But **a true friend will tell you what you have to hear,** what you need to hear, and many times it is not what you want to hear! **A best friend is someone you grow up with. A true friend is someone who helps you grow up!**

I remember watching a movie called, “The Rookie,” and within the scenes there was one that stuck with me. The main character missed his opportunity as a young man to play professional baseball and wound up in a small town coaching a high school team, married with children. He got a second chance much later in life to pitch again and was being scouted for a professional team. He didn’t know what to do at this point in his life as there were mouths to feed and lives to consider other than his own. Throughout the movie it is portrayed that he didn't have much of a relationship with his father, but in this particular scene, he has made his way to his father's house to ask for his advice. He asked his father to help him make the right decision. His dad answered him with these words, **"It's time you started doing what you were created to do and not what you want to do."** Even while we were watching the movie, Cheryl looked over at me and asked, "What does that mean?" I could not answer her because I had no idea what the dad was telling the son! It made no sense to me. Was the dad saying that he was created to play professional baseball, or did he merely want to play professional baseball! I can imagine how frustrated the son in the movie must have been, since it was apparent he left confused as well. Now that I think about it, I see that the father was saying to the son that no one can tell you what to do. Only you know deep inside yourself what you were created to do, and it's time to do it!

It's like this, we are all created with the measure of faith within us and we have a knowing down deep inside our being, but we run around asking everyone else what their opinion is, when we already know what to do and who to be.

Opinion: What do you think I should do about our daughter and her treatment?

Fact: You know what you should do. You have no friend who will stick their neck out this far and you have no earthly father to tell you what he would do, but you do have a heavenly Father who has already put into motion what you know to do.

A true act of faith is trusting God. The act of trust is having faith in an unseen God. Remember faith isn't something you tell someone you have, faith is something you practice when everyone is watching you. Faith is still believing when everything is going wrong, not bragging about it when everything is going right.

I remember hearing my wife say that true faith is being able to rest in the Lord when all others around us are losing their heads. She wrote a book on rest and in it she described true rest as being able to make a decision and laying it at the Father's feet knowing that He is already working on the problem. In fact, He is the answer to every problem! No matter what the outcome, it's in the Father's hands. It's funny, when people don't get what they are asking for, many times they get mad at God. It's like when our children don't get what they want and they throw a tantrum. God sent His Son to the cross of His own free will and decision, so grow up and take responsibility for what God has given you. When you can do that, I believe you will have fulfilled the scripture we already went over in I Corinthians 13:11, *"When I was a child, I spoke as a child, I understood as a child, I thought as a child; but when I became a man, I put away childish things."*

I can become more like God and less like my 'flesh self' in that I can affect more people not by what I get from God, but by what I get out of my relationship with my Father God.

The more of God's image I become like, the less like my old self I am. The more I act like God, the more I look like God. To be God's image means that my life can then reflect His presence wherever and whenever I am with other people. I have heard Cheryl say many times that people will always worship something. People were created to worship something or someone and whatever we worship we become like. My heart's desire is to learn to worship God so fully and faithfully that each day I am allowed to live here on this earth I become more and more like my Creator and less and less like my old unregenerate and unforgiven man. To be regenerated and reborn and forgiven truly means to look like, act like, and be like the one who is forever changing me. The respect I show to my heavenly Father, and my submission to His will for my future is the open door needed for me to be changed forever.

> I wanted more time with my heavenly Father and isn't that what our children want? More time with their father?

Chapter Eleven

For I Have Chosen Him...

Speaking of respect, Cheryl and I have begun to notice an alarming lack of respect for the church and for the institution of family today. When the Spirit of God is moving on people's hearts and they are responding to the altar call, we so often see people who take that moment of reverence as a cue to gather their belongings, scoot to the aisle and head to the door, jingling their car keys. And think about the beginning of the service... during worship how many folks do you see seated with complete disinterest written on their faces, appearing as though there's a thousand other places they'd rather be? And don't tell me you're too tired to stand for twenty minutes of worship, when you'll stand in line for twenty minutes at a restaurant, waiting for a table. The lack of respect for the reverence and holiness of God is truly alarming. Our God is to be revered like none other. Yes, He is our Father, loving, merciful, ever-patient with His children, but make no mistake... HE IS GOD. The beginning of the service is a time of worship. We get to come into the house of worship, God's house, and enter His presence to praise Him and give Him thanks. The end of the service is the time when the altar call is given. The Holy Spirit is ministering to people's hearts and eternal decisions are being made. It's not just a time to prepare to leave the building, it's a time where someone is preparing themselves for eternity, and that should be the most holy time of the entire service. Out of reverence for the move of God and the Holy Spirit, this should be a respected time.

When the president of the United States walks into the room, it is protocol to stand because we honor the office of the president… not the man, but the office. When we pray in church or begin the service, why do some choose to not stand in respect for the King of kings and Lord of lords, whose name is above all names? Shouldn't we honor Him, His name and His house? He is supreme and His very being is to be revered! When we stand for the president, it's not to honor a man because there have been many different men who held the title of president. It's to honor the office of the president of the United States. But when we stand in reverence, to honor our Lord and Savior, Jesus Christ, it's not to honor just the title, but to honor the King of kings and Lord of lords – the only one who ever has or ever will bear that title!

The irreverence for God or lack of respect for Him, the pastor and the house of God doesn't stop there. Disrespect for the mother and father are also rampant in today's society. We remember when our son, Harry III, tried to call his mother, "Cheryl," not

"Mom," "Mama," or any of the names we naturally associate with our mothers. I had a real issue with that. I knew it was some sort of growing up phase, or maybe a burst of independence as he was maturing, but to me, it spelled out very clearly: DISRESPECT. I had to address it and explain to him that I believed a child, no matter what age, simply does not refer to his or her parent by their first name. A child, whether he or she is three or ninety-three, references their parent as "Mom," "Dad," or a variation of one of those names. We should teach our children to use "Sir" and "Ma'am," too! Why? It's simply a matter of respect. To refer to a parent by their first name implies a level of familiarity as would exist between peers and also lends a commonality to the relationship. The child, in this case, our young son, Harry, needed mothering, not a buddy to pass the time with. Remember, a best friend is someone you grew up with but a true friend helps you grow up.

I want you to know here that as I have gotten older and the boys are grown they still call me "Dad" or "Pops," and even when I play basketball with them they call me "O.G." for "Old Guy." Now you might say that is disrespectful... no, disrespectful is when one of the young men playing out on the court one day called me "Old Man." He persisted calling me "Old Man" until finally I took enough of it and said,

"You can call me Pop, Dad, O.G. or even Preacher, but I don't like being called Old Man." The funny part was when one of his teammates came over to him and said, "I wouldn't be calling him 'Old Man' because that 'old man' is schooling you!"

I remember a scene in the movie "Big Jake" with John Wayne. He and his son were reunited after a long breech in their relationship. The two ended up in a fight and it stemmed from the fact that the grown son insisted upon calling John Wayne's character, Jacob McCandles, "Daddy." Now you might say what was wrong with that? Well, it wasn't the "Daddy," it was the tone. And after the fight John Wayne said to his son, "You can call me Father, Jake, or Mr. McCandles, and (something else I won't quote) but if you ever call me Daddy again I'll finish this fight!" Now I don't like the fight part but the lack of respect or reverence and the son's tone was what was being noted here. Likewise, I needed to make that same strong point with our son. We had our conversation about respecting and honoring his mama and he quickly changed his course. To this day, at twenty-five years old, Harry is a young man who recognizes authority and who has a strong reverence for his God, his family, and his mama and daddy. He's a great young man, not perfect, but who is? And he is respectful. If the lesson early in his young life had gone unaddressed, or had been labeled as, 'cute,' I wonder what other 'cute' irreverencies may have been allowed to blossom and grow in our son's life?

Can you see how quickly and how easily a young life can take a shift in a certain direction? There are a number of TV shows that I was told to watch when I was writing this book so I've glimpsed at them lately, where troubled young people are taken into an actual prison system for a day, and they are forced to basically live out a day in the life of a true-to-life prisoner. Many of the prisoners who were placed behind bars in their teens, are middle-aged now, never having lived what you and I consider a normal life. When the prisoners have a sit-down, face to face conversation with the young people, they almost always say that they wish someone would have taken authority over them, showed them the error of their ways and put a stop to what they were doing. Want to know what else they say to these young people who are on the verge of ending up where they are, in prison? They tell them to respect their parents, their teachers and themselves. Two things come to mind in regards to these TV shows, the story of Harry III choosing to call his mama, "Cheryl," and this very book I wrote for you, with its subtitle, *Longing for a Father*.

Longing for a Father

First, is it possible, in some of these prisoners' lives, that small, seemingly insignificant little irreverencies were allowed to go unchecked? I mean, surely, there was some sort of turning point, some sort of game-changer for the folks who ended up facing a lifetime in prison, right? Could it have begun with something as 'insignificant' as being allowed to hit or slap someone when they were babies? Maybe they started calling their mom by her first name, then their father became their "Old Man"? Where does it stop? Behind bars at nineteen because up to now you had always gotten away with everything, you were unstoppable, you were bullet-proof, and then you took a life, or forced someone to do something unthinkable against their will, or bought or sold something illegal, or stole something you thought you deserved to have? You know, it's so cute, some of the things that babies and young children do when they are asserting their independence, but those things have to be brought in check before they establish a pattern within that child. Who will need to bring those things into check?

Longing...
for a
Father

This brings me to the second thing that came to mind when I saw the TV show about the young people being exposed to prison life.

Who will guide the children and bring their budding independence into check before it becomes a rampaging irreverent lack of respect for authority, God, family, and even themselves? **The father.** Men, God has ordained us as His warriors for His daughters (yes, that's your wife... she is His daughter) and for His babies. We should stand when our wives or our mothers get up from the table – our sons will learn it and our daughters will expect it. It's all about respect, good manners and respect. Men, our children are a gift from Him, a blessing that He has entrusted us to bring up in the *"... training and admonition of the Lord."*

Ephesians 6:4

And you, fathers, do not provoke your children to wrath, but bring them up in the training and admonition of the Lord.

I looked up several translations of this scripture and found varying words for *training* and *admonition* (instruction, discipline, nurture, chastening, teaching, correction). Please do not misunderstand or take my words (I took them from the Bible, so they are God's words), to mean something that they **do not mean**. There is no implication to be made here. I am interpreting scripture for my own life and for my own family and I trust God's Word to be

100% true and 100% good. Yes, words like 'discipline' and 'correction' can be used in some extreme contexts, but I am in no way endorsing harsh punishment types, cruelty, over-correction or any other cruel or unusual punishment for children. YOU NEVER RAISE YOUR HAND TO A CHILD OR STRIKE A CHILD EVER!! In fact, that's a sure-fire way to accomplish the opposite of the goal here, which is RESPECT. Giving it, getting it, teaching it, learning it, and living it.

RESPECT
Giving it,
getting it,
teaching it,
learning it,
living it.

Listen, one translation says:

Ephesians 6:4 (Weymouth New Testament)

And you, fathers, do not irritate your children, but bring them up tenderly with true Christian training and advice.

Bring them up tenderly. God is LOVE. Love and nurture your children, guiding them in the *"...training and admonition of the Lord,"* and they will grow and mirror you, their father, in love, nurture and respect. Teach them, by your words and by your actions, to show respect; give it where it is due, and it is due to the ones who brought you into this world, your mother and your father. And it is emphatically due to the ONE who brought us all into this world, our heavenly Father.

Remember, Matthew 6:21 states that, *"Where your treasure is, there your heart will be also."*

It's all about the heart and honoring the Father out of respect for what He sent His Son to do for us. Manners and respect. Respect not for the office of the father, but respect for the Father of all mankind.

The last verse in Malachi says there will be a reconciliation of the fathers to the children. The reconciliation will be produced by repentance.

Malachi 4:6 (KJV)

And he shall turn the heart of the fathers to the children, and the heart of the children to their fathers, lest I come and smite the earth with a curse.

Having a repentant heart means to humble yourself and ask for forgiveness, and to say, "I was wrong." When you and I have a repentant heart, there will be a reconciliation of the family.

II Chronicles 7:14 says, "... *if my people who are called by My name will humble themselves, and pray and seek My face, and turn from their wicked ways, I will hear from heaven, and will forgive their sin and heal their land."*

Humility brings a repentant heart and repentance brings the heavenly Father back into the equation.

Genesis 18:19 (NIV)

For I have chosen him, so that he will direct his children and his household after him to keep the way of the LORD by doing what is right and just, so that the LORD will bring about for Abraham what he has promised him."

Different translations use this terminology in regards to the father's role in child-rearing:

"For I know him, that he will command his children and his household after him, and they shall keep the way of the LORD, to do justice and judgment..." (KJV)

"I have singled him out..." (New Living Translation)

Men, God states that He has **chosen** you. He **knows** you will complete this task and He has **singled** you out. What a vote of confidence our Father has in us as men, His warriors as fathers! It's time to become God's man – the man He has called and created you to be!

It's humbling, but don't forget the truest form of humility was when Jesus Christ came to this earth as a man and went to the cross and died for us. He humbled Himself in front of all humanity and was crucified. He could have saved Himself from that humiliation they put Him through, the mocking and beating, being spit on and eventually being crucified. Even at the cross, one of the thieves being crucified next to Him said, (paraphrasing) "If You are the Messiah then why don't You save Yourself?" Why? Love and humility, that's why. John 3:16 states, "*For God so loved the world that He gave His only begotten Son...*" And Jesus loved you so much that He gave Himself up for you. Men, it's all about love. Do nothing from fractional motives, but out of love. If love isn't in it, then you are not rearing or correcting your children God's way. His way of loving is about giving not getting, giving love and then because of your giving, love comes in return, because you loved them first. Just like Jesus. He loved us first, before we ever knew Him. Now that's real love; that's true love. That's the love of a father.

Genesis 18:19 (NIV)

For I have chosen him, so that he will direct his children and his household after him to keep the way of the LORD by doing what is right and just..."

Chapter Twelve

It Ain't Easy…

Okay, here is my last thought on the subject of 'when I became a man.' I want to discuss what the ancient definition in the Hebrew language says about *man*. Well, actually the ancient Hebrew does not even use the word [3]*man* in the context of the gender of man, but rather *male/husband. Man* in itself refers to *the species of God's own image*, and it is gendered both male and female to complete the picture.

What we consider the word [3]*man* to mean, the male gender, is actually *male/husband*. In Hebrew, the word for *male* is the exact same word for *husband*. It is the word *ish*. In the ancient Hebrew it means, *his hand is in the midst of the fire*. Okay, what fire? Our God is an all-consuming fire! That is the fire that men *(male/husband)* are to have their hands within at all times. We, as God's men, are to have our hand within Him, His purifying fire at all times!

So God created us as men, male men and potential husbands for His glory in relationships. Just as He created us as *male/husbands,* He also created women as *female/wives*. He designed us to be husbands so we could go forth and procreate and bring forth the next generation of children in godly households which we call families. So, realizing that He created us *male/husband* not merely man, male is the gender God created and man is the species; but understanding that God created us *male/husband* reveals that the scripture referring to *"When I became a man,"* means that as a male I have a choice to grow up and become a mature man!

Father in the ancient Hebrew means *strong leader of the home.*

We have free will and we can choose to become a man which means acting and responding and taking on the responsibility of the man's role in society, families, and relationships. This responsibility also includes the evolution of husband into the role of father whether children are birthed from you or not.

[3]***Father* in the ancient Hebrew means *strong leader of the home.*** So whether we bring children into our lives through birth, adoption, foster care, etc. it does not matter. Biologically being able to plant the seed that produces children does not give you the characteristics of a God-kind of father. Taking on the nature of a mature male, whose life is being developed and shaped by the

ultimate of fathers, God Himself, is what makes us true fathers. *Father* means *strong leader of the home.* That means strong in faith, in faithfulness, in relationships and mostly, strong in maturity and leadership.

[3]*Anger* and *hatred* are two ancient Hebrew words that give us a true picture of what being a God-kind of father is all about. ***Anger* and *hatred* are defined as *the closed heart/hand of a father*, or simply put, *without fathering.*** We have a generation of men and women who have been reared without true and godly leadership in the home. Without strong leadership in the home from a male perspective, we have anger and hatred as seed growing within the next generation.

We can undo this but it is not easy. Once these roots have grown and taken root in a heart it is difficult to pull them all up and get them out. It is not impossible but it is difficult. Only the true love of a father can undo and root out these seeds of anger and hatred, which gives us the definition of *love* in the ancient Hebrew language. [3]***Love* means *the father revealed.*** *Love* is the opposite of *anger/hatred. Love is the open hand of a father.* When children are reared in homes where the father figure is accessible, easy to get to and be with, then the heart and hand of the father is open towards the children. The father being available and open to the home, the wife and the children, is so very important that it is literally the definition of love within the home and family!

Maybe that is why in Ephesians 5, the chapter in the Bible which is the guideline and instruction chapter of love/home/marriage between a man and a woman, it says three different times for the man to *love* his wife. Love seems to come more naturally for a woman than it does for a man, or at least the 'showing of love' comes easier for most women than for most men. God chose to tell us as men, repeatedly to love, love, love, our wives. This is the open heart, the open hand, love revealed to the wife and children in our lives. Without this love, anger and hatred begin to grow within their hearts and whether we want to receive the blame for it or not, the buck stops with us!

> Anger and hatred cannot be 'gotten rid of.' They can only be replaced... *by love.*

Many people have spent their lives trying to rid their emotions of unhealthy anger issues and having feelings of hatred in their hearts. When we researched these words and saw these powerful truths in Hebrew, the most ancient of languages, that the Bible was originally written in, we began to see a great truth. [3]*Anger and hatred cannot be 'gotten rid of.' They can only be replaced, by love.* Love bears all things, love endures all things, love hardly notices when done wrong. Love never fails. (I Corinthians 13:4-7) Anger cannot be taken out of a person, but rather a person can fill themselves up so full with the love of Father God, that anger and hatred are literally displaced!

Once love takes over and fills one's life completely, then there is no longer any room for anger or hatred. It's truly a lifelong choice to receive love which in turn undoes all the deep roots of anger and hatred, replacing within one's heart the ability to give out what they are now full of. I have heard Cheryl say for many years that all people 'manifest what they are full of.' Whatever we fill our lives up with is what is going to come out when we get squeezed, or knocked around. Whatever is the overflowing part of our lives is what spills out at all times. It comes out our mouths, our body language, the way we walk, talk, think, and act.

Just as light and dark cannot cohabitate in the same space neither can love and hate coexist together. We are either walking in love or we are manifesting what we are full of with hate coming out every orifice of our being. We must take responsibility for our emotional health as well as every other aspect of who we are. We can never impart to our children who we are not. We can never give to our children what we don't own in our personal lives. I want to give love to my children, but I cannot give what I do not receive. That's why knowing the love of God made manifest in our lives is crucial to being the kind of father we long to be. Without knowing the ultimate of all fathers, how can we even pretend to be one ourselves?

Chapter Thirteen

The True Meaning of Longing

Three months after our daughter died of a brain tumor, Cheryl was diagnosed with colon cancer. I can honestly say I found myself confused, frustrated and not just a little angry. I guess I'm not using the correct word. As I mentioned before, I was wounded within every ounce of my being, but I was not really angry. I was just plain mad! I couldn't seem to catch a break and all the old feelings of rejection and abandonment were closing in on my heart. I felt like God had forgotten me. I felt like God had moved on to some other family and had left me and mine behind. Sometimes I felt numb and other times, I felt like every part of me was a raw, oozing sore of pain and heartbreak.

I was sitting in church mad. It bears repeating the difference that I believe exists between being 'mad' and being 'angry.' I believe being mad at God is okay. We get mad at our earthly fathers or sons, but at the end of the day, we still are fathers and sons. A strong relationship can handle somebody getting mad. Anger is a different issue altogether. Anger puts down a root and is joined by bitterness and hatred. We need to deal with anger before it manifests into something greater. It's a slippery slope and you don't want to go down it! Neither did I!

But I can honestly say that I was mad, because I was! I didn't want to be in church, but I didn't want to give anybody a chance to make a comment about me, or say that we were not faithful. I didn't want to hide either. We had been judged pretty harshly by so-called church folks, especially Word of Faith charismatic types. I say this carefully, as we are Word of Faith charismatic people, also. I mean the Bible is plain about faith. It is impossible to please God without faith. Therefore I have to say that we are faith people, because we want to always please God. These were religious Word of Faith people that were judging us. I want to be clear here that only a handful were judging us, but you know, the **few** is what we focus on. Our children do the same thing, don't they? They focus on the one thing they did wrong, instead of remembering all the things they've done right. Tell your child what they did right today.

I had people walk right up to me, look me straight in the face at our daughter's funeral and tell me that they knew why our daughter had died. When I inquired as to the answer to this question their reply was, "Because you didn't have enough faith for her healing."

A man at Gabrielle's funeral actually walked up to me and said, "I've watched your ministry for years, and I am going to be watching to see how you get through this one." He was not being encouraging at all – he was being harsh with his remarks.

Several churches cancelled our already scheduled meetings in their churches with no explanations. Those particular churches have stayed away from us even now after eleven years. After Cheryl was diagnosed with cancer three months after Gabrielle went to heaven, people came up to me and said that our family was under a curse. Well, that made me feel warm and fuzzy all over! We got letters and phone calls, and people walking up to us more often than not with strange comments and phrases.

Some people told Cheryl that when we returned home (we were on the road at the time doing extended meetings), if she would go to the cemetery Gabrielle would be standing by her grave, alive and well. You and I both know that is ridiculous – absolute crazy talk! But when we got home, Cheryl just had to go to the cemetery no matter how foolish she knew she was being. She said the entire way there she talked to the Lord and told Him she knew that Gabrielle would not be there, but she said that she had to settle this once and for all. She drove out there, and got out of her car, and she told me that she said out loud, "I knew you would not be here, for why would you ever come back to this earth after walking the streets of gold with Jesus?"

That was it for Cheryl. She has never been back to this day. She is that kind of a lady. She draws a line in the sand and never looks back, and that is what she did. She heard the Lord say to her, "Gabrielle is not in your past, but she is in your future." That was the dividing line separating past and future for her. She has never looked back since then.

I found myself that day in church with so many questions and absolutely no answers.

I found myself that day in church with so many questions and absolutely no answers. I didn't even know where to begin to ask to find the peace that I needed to go on with our lives. I was talking to God and like I said, I was mad and really frustrated. I was focusing on all the things that I didn't have in my life and I was learning how to complain, quite effortlessly. God is so amazing and wonderful. He is the only one we can complain to, who won't get fed up with us and walk away or get disgusted with us. My Father God spoke to my heart and said these words to me, "Son, what is really bothering you?" I told Him that I missed my daughter. That's when

He said to me, "How much do you miss her?" I said, "Lord, I long for her." The Father said, "How much do you long for her?" I answered Him, "I long for her so much it hurts."

At that moment, the Lord reminded me of a question someone had asked me about how you know when you are really in love with your wife. I remember telling the person who asked me that question, "Remember before you married your wife, when you were not with her how you could not wait to be with her again?" The man said that he did remember that feeling. I told him that at that point, "You longed to be with her to the point that it hurt. Remember?" The man said that he did remember those exact feelings. I explained to him that pull of the feelings of longing describes what true love is. "When you long for her, the pull of that longing causes you to want to be with her more than anywhere else in the world."

The Lord said to my spirit, "You love Gabrielle so much that being separated from her causes you to long to be with her." I answered Him, "Yes, that's right." The Lord said, "Your purpose from this day forth is to tell My people **if they would long for Me as much as you long for your daughter, then I'll come quicker.** But they don't long for Me, and they don't miss Me. That's why I have not returned yet. They talk to Me and they talk to Me, but they are so busy with their own lives and their struggles that they don't really spend time with Me. The only reason they even come to Me is because they want Me to get them out of trouble or for Me to meet their needs. They only come to Me because they have to; they have nowhere else to go. They are not pulling Me towards them to come quickly. The last thing Jesus told them was that He is coming; He is coming; He is coming. The church's response is supposed to be, 'Even so, come quickly, Lord Jesus.' But this is not what the church is saying. The bride of Christ has not found her voice and until she does..." His voice trailed off but I caught the message. I understood for the first time that His delay in coming was not because of His withholding His affection from us. His delay was because of us, His bride, His church, withholding our affection from Him.

> Our Father God longs for us, but do we long for Him?

I knew immediately what the message of my heart would be from that day forth. I know how much I longed for Gabrielle and I could only imagine how much the Father God must long for us, His children. My heart broke that day with the realization that our Father God longs for us, but we don't long for Him. Is it any wonder that He has not returned to take us home with Him?

My desire to be with my daughter is not because I have to, it's because I want to be with her. *I long for her!* I don't have to be with our children here on the earth, *I want to be with them.* It is not a requirement; it is a pleasure, a joy to be with them! As I have traveled this road these last few years, I realize that I don't even long for my earthly dad any more. He has been gone to heaven for some forty years and time has helped the longing feelings. I'm not saying that there are not times when I miss him. I do. These are usually times when I need his counsel, or his advice, times when an earthly father's words sure would come in handy. But to be factual, I don't know what earthly counsel from a father really is because I never had it. I guess you can't miss what you never have had. There was a time in my life when older men would try to be a father figure to me but I resented it and would say to them, "Where were you when I needed a dad?"

That's why I have worked so hard to be there for our sons in a deep and meaningful relationship. It gives me pleasure when they ask me for counsel and advice. That brought a great revelation to me of how our Father God must feel when we come to

Him with a true need for His help. I am learning now as I have two sons, how to be the counselor.

When it comes to my earthly dad, I don't really miss him anymore. Maybe that's because I have developed a Father/son relationship with my heavenly Father. Maybe it is because I have come to recognize that I can spend time with my heavenly Father and not have to have the physical proximity of a person with me. When I am in God's presence I feel His love, His warmth, His guidance, His encouragement and all of that is so much more than a physical human being in the room with me.

> Spend time with your children or someone else will.

Even though I have grown to this place in my relationship does not mean that I don't need people relationships. I do. Sometimes I just need somebody that I can physically see and touch, too.

Our children need us. They need us to be actually present, on the scene and paying attention. Being there for them is so very important! Consider this little saying when it comes to spending time with your children, "If not you, then who?"

Humanity seems to always be in a rush. People seem to be on a timeline, a 'get to the point, I'm in a hurry' attitude and this is with people who love you! Most people can't wait to leave or change the subject. Many people can't deal with hearing all our problems, but the Father God never seems to tire of us. He longs for me, and He wants to be with me, and I am learning to long for Him, and want to be with Him, too. Not because I need something from Him, but because I want to be with Him, simply for no reason at all. Just to be with Him is so wonderful, without an agenda, or even a request.

The heavenly Father longs for His time to be with us as we long to be with Him and that statement alone should let you know how much God loves each one of us! **Just think, the God who created the heavens and the earth, who literally flung the stars from His fingertips and scooped out the oceans with His hands wants to spend as much time with us as we will give Him! That's how special we are to our heavenly Father.**

Yes, He is God but He has given us the ability to talk with Him daily and the cool thing is that the same God who flung the stars and scooped out the oceans loves us, really loves us and longs for us. He wants us to talk to Him, and He takes the time to talk back to us. Our God answers our prayers!

Oh, and just so you know, I long for my wife, after twenty-six years of being married to her, after only a few hours apart. I can hardly imagine how much God must love and long for us!

> I can only imagine how much God loves and longs for us!

Chapter Fourteen

Leaving a Legacy of Longing

I have had the idea for this book for a long time, for almost ten years to be exact. Ever since I first heard those words, "If My children would long for Me as much as you long for your daughter, then I'll come quicker." Now don't get all 'theologian-y' on me and say that there is nothing we can do to get Jesus back sooner. Don't start writing me letters with, *"But of that day and hour no one knows..."* Save yourself the stamp. I know what Mark 13:32 says.

"But of that day and hour no one knows, not even the angels in heaven, nor the Son, but only the Father."

I know some other things too, like we are a church body that is quite 'cool' in our relationship as a whole with the Father God. 'Passion' would not be the first word that comes to my mind to describe the ongoing love affair of God's people with their beloved Savior, Jesus Christ. I know that God knows everything, past, present and future. God knows the future long before we get to it. God not only knows the future but He has already been to our future and knows what we are going to choose. Okay, I got that deep thought from Cheryl, who is the deep thinker in our house, but hey, I have heard her say it so much, I am actually beginning to understand it! God knows all things. We do not know much of anything. If you think you do, then you are already dumber than you think you are! I have said this for many years, **if you think you are the smartest person in the room, then you have just identified the dumbest one!** People are not talking about you because you are smart, but because you 'think' you are! The statement, "If My children would long for Me as much as you long for your daughter, then I'll come quicker," was spoken to my heart at a time when I was contemplating my future, my reason for being and questioning whether I had failed my daughter and my family because she did not get healed and died. I felt such guilt, like I had opened the door to this horrible thing, somewhere, but I had no idea where that could have been! I felt guilty, that somehow I, as the head of the household, could have prevented this tragedy in our lives. I felt that somehow, if I had been a different man, Gabrielle would not have gotten sick and died and Cheryl would not have gotten cancer. Now I realize that these thoughts are not even logical. I realize that we humans actually get the idea that we control things here on this earth. There is definitely a great deal of merit to the concept of choices. God does set choices before us, but He also told us what to choose. He said for us to choose life. We did choose life. Gabrielle chose life. We spoke it, we prayed it, we believed it and we even received it. But not like

> LIFE that God sets before us is ETERNAL.

we thought about life. Life for us was actually living on this earth, in this thing we call a body, but is nothing more than an earth suit. *Life that God sets before us is eternal.* Eternal life, yeah, that's it. That's the choice we can make, and we have made it. Gabrielle chose eternal life, that's why she is in our future, because she is alive and well and not living on planet earth but rather living, *really living,* eternally in heaven. We choose life, too. We hope to live on this earth as long as necessary to accomplish and fulfill God's eternal plan for us. While we are living in these earth suits we are learning about truth, and faithfulness, and life – real life. We are learning that life is eternal; there is no stopping place, no jumping off place, no 'end of the line.' Eternal life is simply that, *eternal.* That's what we choose and we choose it for eternity.

I want you to focus on the statement about **longing** which means, **'a strong desire.'**

[1]long·ing
-noun

: a strong desire especially for something unattainable:

> The Lord said to Cheryl, "If you focus on what you don't have, you will lose what you do have."

At that time in my life I needed a strong desire so that I would stop sitting around feeling sorry for myself. I needed a new focus and I found it on Christmas morning, 1999. Gabrielle had passed to heaven just one month earlier, and Cheryl was sick. I remember, she was so very physically sick. We didn't know it yet, but she had cancer. It was Christmas day and Cheryl was trying so hard to have a good day with our sons. She heard the Lord say to her heart, "If you focus on what you don't have, you will lose what you do have." And there it was, plain and simple. It was not easy but it was simple. When we focused on Gabrielle who had moved to heaven, more than we focused on our sons who were still here with us on earth, God was warning us that we were in jeopardy of losing them! We had to focus on them; we had to pay attention and listen and learn from them. We had to build a strong relationship with them, individually and as a family, without Gabrielle. We didn't like it, not then or now, but it is what it is.

That was huge when she told me what the Lord had given her. It also confirmed the statement the Lord had given her that Gabrielle is not in our past but she is in our future. God always confirms His words. He never contradicts Himself. He never brings confusion or chaos to our minds and hearts. He brings peace. His words will always bring rest and peace. Even when we don't like what He is saying, we will still feel peace when we receive His words!

So the challenge began to not look back, to focus ahead and into the future, to pay attention to those with us. This was a huge revelation for us – don't look back. It can be a huge revelation for you too, but you will have to practice it the rest of your life starting today, and then tomorrow, and the next day, and well, yeah, every other day after that too.

The second thing I got was to look to the future, think about the future, focus on the future. It was not only the fact that Gabrielle was already in heaven waiting for us, but that we could join her there eventually when it is our time to cross over to heaven. There will be a huge family reunion! Every day between now and then we must wake up and be grateful for what we have, and who we have, and not grieve or be upset for what we don't have now.

It was a great revelation that helped us move forward but it was a walk of faith, and one we were going to quickly need. Cheryl was diagnosed with cancer only three months after we buried Gabrielle. The statement of "If you focus on what you don't have, you will lose what you do have" became a huge reality for me. I have my two sons, and I have my wife. Don't focus on missing Gabrielle, who is alive and well and living in heaven for all of eternity. We will be together again, eternally, and we will not be separated. I had to make myself see what was right in front of me.

I began to realize that what we allow our minds to rehearse over and over again can cause our future to be bright or dismal. My choice in the matter, the question for me was what was I going to rehash on a continual basis on the 'instant replay' big screen of my mind? I realized that what I had in the room every day was very important to me for that day. I had to retrain my mind to focus on each day individually, and learn to be thankful for each day. After the long battle we had fought for Gabrielle to live, the physical result was her death, but I had to learn to not look back and stop rehearsing what was behind me that could not be changed. If each day we got through, we managed to do so without a huge tragedy, and could lay our heads down at night without someone dying, then that day, that 24 hour period, was a good day.

I know this may sound horrible, or morbid to you as a reader, but you have to remember we fought back death every day for almost a year with Gabrielle, and then there was only one week between her funeral and when Cheryl began having severe symptoms of sickness in her body. We were not living per se, we were in a war, and we were simply surviving daily. So once again, if we got to the evening and we could lay our heads on the pillow and no one had died that day, then it was a good day.

I'm not saying that it's easy to not replay the bad things. In fact, it's very difficult not to! The bad things are easier to remember, easier to let come flooding into our minds and out of our mouths, but that does not get us to where we want to be in the future. My wife had a lifetime of bad things happen to her that she could replay and relive. She was crippled from a car wreck and told she may never walk again. When she did walk, she had a short leg for six years, and the after-effects of a cracked back. She had been through three windshields with her face and had numerous other injuries over the years. She had been diagnosed with more diseases than most people have even heard of but the Lord has delivered her out of them all!

> There is not one excuse from our past that should ever excuse our present choices.

I could spend the rest of my life focusing on the fact that my father died when I was ten years old or that our daughter died at the age of six years old. I could try and use those things as an excuse for every wrong choice I ever made in life like some people I know do, but that is not an excuse. Choose you this day, today, whom you will serve, what direction you will go, and what you believe. No matter what has happened to us, no matter what life has thrown at us, there are never enough excuses to explain away our unwise and bad choices. Rehearsing those past situations and circumstances will never cause the future to be different. Only by seeing into the future with faith eyes, and believing that what is in front of us does not have to be predicted by what is behind us, can we move forward into a victorious life ahead.

Jesus states in the book of John, chapter 16, verse 33, *"I have told you these things, so that in Me you may have [perfect] peace and confidence. In the world you have tribulation and trials and distress and frustration; but be of good cheer [take courage; be confident, certain, undaunted]! For I have overcome the world. [I have* ***deprived*** *it of power to harm you and have conquered it for you.]."* (AMP) Simply stated, Jesus was telling those of us who read those words now, just like He was speaking to those present at that moment, that this world in itself is hard. It is not easy, it will have problems, and situations, and circumstances. It will be troublesome and frustrating and distressing. There will be days that are depressing and want to make us run away as fast as possible. But He also said that we could be happy even in the worst of situations once we realize that our joy and happiness, and even our cheer is not based upon our surroundings, or our circumstances or our situations. Our cheer, happiness, and joy are based in our eternal knowledge of who we truly are in Christ Jesus!

You might be saying to yourself, "How can you tell me you want me to be happy in the situation I am in right now?" All I can give you is my definition of real faith. Our faith was questioned; I felt that *my* faith especially was questioned. Even more so than my wife's or my children's faith, but as head of the household, my faith was in question in many people's minds. Faith is not something you brag about when everything is going great in your life. Faith is not trying to have someone determine how much faith you have or how faithful you are because the Bible says in Romans 12:3 that we all have the measure of faith.

For I say, through the grace given to me, to everyone who is among you, not to think of himself more highly than he ought to think, but to think soberly, as God has dealt to each one a measure of faith.

Faith is not fo
a season.
Faith is eterna
It has a
beginning, bu
it never ends.

Faith is not something someone can physically see, or touch, or taste or smell, or hear in our lives. But faith does become visible when all hell breaks loose in our lives. In fact, I define faith as, "When all hell breaks loose in your life and you still believe." Faith is not just a bumper sticker that reads, 'I'VE GOT FAITH!' Faith is when you continue believing, no matter what is going wrong in your life. Faith is continuing to believe when everyone else has decided to stop believing. Faith does not have a '.' (period) at the end of it, but rather an arrow on the line we call infinity. Faith does not have a stopping place, or an ending. Faith is not for a season or a timeline. Faith goes on and on no matter what the outcome for a particular reason, event, life, problem, situation or circumstance. Faith is eternal, it has a definite beginning but it truly has no end. **Faith is simply put in two words, "I believe."**

I want you to know that as I write this I am not saying that I don't have tough days. I do have very tough days. Even after more than a decade, the pain is still there. I am not saying that I don't continually miss and long for our daughter, because I do. But there is a difference now in it; there is a shifting of the emotional response to the memories. Where once there was only heart-wrenching pain and tears that accompanied each thought and memory, now many times there is laughter, fond memories, and funny stories that come along for the ride.

Now I can remember such fun times, like bedtime in our house. Gabrielle was never one to sleep in her own room, or even in her own bed. We were not the type of parents that allowed our children to sleep in our bed but for some reason, and thank God we didn't resist it, Gabrielle slept most of her life between us in the bed. And don't think this was just a Gabrielle thing or a special little girl thing. Nope. The boys had sleeping bags and we had sleepovers in our room at the foot of our bed many nights. That's possibly why they still come in and sit with us before bedtime even now.

But we started out as we had with our sons, trying to train her to sleep in her own bed. We would go through the bedtime ritual which could be long and drawn out at the Salem home. Much reading time, story time, and even long prayer time, too, could last between one and two hours nightly. We didn't mind, because we got to know the children's thoughts during these hours, and we got to hear their hearts as they prayed each evening. But eventually, it was time to lie down and go to sleep.

The boys were good about it, but Gabrielle was more difficult. We would read, pray, sing and even play a little longer trying to convince her to settle down each evening. Finally we would get her into her bed, and here would come the long drawn out conversations. We would try to leave the room but she would say, "Daddy, don't leave." Cheryl would ask her why we could not leave and Gabrielle would say that she did not want to be alone. Of course, Cheryl would give her the spiritual answer of, "Gabrielle, you are never alone. Jesus is always with you." But that would never satisfy that quick mind of hers. She would quickly reply, "But I want somebody in here with skin on them."

Now how could you argue with that? I mean, the boys had each other in their room, and Cheryl and I had each other in our room, it didn't seem quite fair that she had to be alone when everyone else had someone with skin on them! Of course, that always resulted in her winding up between us in our bed. We didn't mind at all really, and thank God we had those extra hours with her. Watching her go to sleep and watching her wake up each and every day of her life for six years cannot be taken from us.

I pray that as you are making your way through these pages that God is revealing to you a deeper relationship with Him as your true heavenly Father. But I also, remind you if you have children, **do not neglect the time you spend with them. You can never get back those hours, days, weeks, months and years you didn't invest in them.** Now is the time to give all you can find in your time each and every day to those relationships all around you that you long to have for eternity. Your mate and your children are investments of your time, and there is a huge promise of a long-term return. Stay with it and don't get discouraged. If you have missed the boat on this but those you love are still around, then go to them, and repent. Tell them you now see the importance of it, and ask them to let you prove to them for the rest of your life how much you long to be with them. People are much more forgiving than we give them credit for most of the time. And relationships can grow from any point, even this one, right now, right here.

I pray that as
you are
making your
way through
these pages
that God is
revealing to
you a deeper
relationship
with Him as
your heavenly
Father.

Chapter Fifteen

If Not for My Father

I am thankful for my earthly father and mother. I am thankful that they continued to have children past the first and then the second as I am the third child, and the baby of our family. As thankful as I am for my father, he was, simply put, just that... a father. He was a good provider, but he was not a dad, not really. I am not mad at my father, nor am I ashamed to tell you that he was a workaholic, because he was. I've already mentioned that my father was a marine and a good one at that. I also mentioned that he was the son of an immigrant from the Middle East. He was taught as a young man that your self-worth was determined by what you have and what you achieve in life. He was taught that the things you acquire in life determine your position in the future and that a good man, a good husband, and a great father provides for his family above all else. My father did exactly that; he was a great provider.

My very first book was influenced by this and I called it, *For Men Only... Not Just Provider but Participant*. My father's success in business was great, even to the fact that when he died, Ford Motor Company sent a brand new Lincoln hearse and a string of black Lincoln cars for his funeral.

During the funeral procession to his final resting place, the route was altered so we could drive past my father's dealership as that was where he spent most of his time.

The Bible plainly states in Matthew 6:21, *"For where your treasure is, there your heart will be also."* My father's treasure was his business because he spent most of his life there. Now before you go and say that he was a bad father or that I am a resentful son, make sure you listen fully to all that I am saying. I am stating the facts and the truth about it. I refuse to be the kind of person that pretends like things were perfect when they were not, and I also refuse to be the kind of person that allows those things that either happened or didn't happen in my past to predict my future.

My father's way of expressing his love for his family was to provide more for us than what he had in his life. His love language was provision. It is also one of God's love languages and is expressed in one of His many names, *Jehovah Jireh, my provider, my provision.* My father definitely had this one characteristic of the nature of God in his personal life. He was generous with paying for gifts and wanted us to have the best. Notice I said he was a generous payer, not necessarily a generous giver.

His way was to call the store and make provision of how to pay for what we needed. This was his way of taking care of us and this he did very well. He loved us. He found his joy in watching us when he was at home, which was not very often. One thing he did was have me come to work with him every Saturday morning to see what he was creating for me to take over in the future. I was a six-year-old little boy wearing a sport coat, tie, white shirt, and gray pants to work! Today they might call it 'child labor abuse' but then he called it 'on the job training,' preparing me for my future and spending time with his son!

My dad at his office.

I cherished those Saturdays and I still love the thought of sitting in the front seat dressed just like my father, right down to the tasseled shoes, going off to work. It's no different than a baseball player who lets his son in the locker room, introducing him to the sport by association, by being around the players, at the field, and even on the field. It's the old adage, "You reap what you sow." My father wanted me to reap the knowledge necessary to carry on in his footsteps the business he was building. I was supposed to follow in his footsteps and become a success for my family by hard work. So some would say these were good lessons; some would say that he didn't play ball with me. It all depends on how you look at it, and what you want to focus on in life.

My mother took us to church every Sunday. We didn't miss church, ever. What was my dad's way of going to church with us? Mother would dress us up in our Sunday best and we would be sitting in the church, all lined up on the pew. Here would come my father, riding by the window on the riding lawn mower as he mowed the grass during the service. In his mind, he went to church with us. He was there, on the premises, I'll give him that. My fondest memories of these times now are the thoughts of my mom forbidding us to even glance over at him as he continually went by, over and over again! The worst pinch in my life would come if my eyes wandered over to that window! My mother was so embarrassed about it all, but somehow I knew she understood his way.

So good lessons or bad lessons, I guess that depends on how you look at it, or in my case, how I look at it, from a small child's point of view. At the time, that was my life, and it was cool. I can honestly say now, that I missed my father watching me play baseball. I can honestly say I miss the fact that my father never took me down to the store to help me pick out my glove either. I remember asking him for a new glove one time when I was going to play little league and instead of him taking me to buy it, he simply said, "Tomorrow your mother will take you to Yankee's store and you ask for the manager. He will put a glove in your hand that is the best one. I will make arrangements for payment." I still have that glove to this day.

That was his way. In my dad's eyes, he accomplished the task that was set before him. He bought the glove, and I got a new glove. Even on our little league shirts (in those days you had a sponsor who paid for your uniforms) on the back of our shirts it said Salem Lincoln Mercury. That was my dad's way of being a part of my little league experience. He bought the uniforms. All was well.

For some, this is a sad story but for me, it is a great lesson that I have not forgotten for many decades. I know through my father's actions what not to do for my children. I look at the 'bad' things my dad did or didn't do in life as a learning experience, kind of like on the job training, which he truly believed in.

I had an opportunity to talk with a man who was very influential and famed in his profession. I watched his life and read his books and learned so much from his life experiences. When I had the opportunity to meet him I told him that I had enjoyed and learned from his life. He asked me which of his life's experiences had taught me the most. I know he was thinking that I was going to flatter him with one of his great achievements, of which there were many. I could have told him many things from the great success stories throughout his lifetime but the honest answer was probably not the one he was expecting. I told him that one of the greatest lessons I had learned from him was from one of his greatest failures. His sharing that experience had taught me more than all his greatest victories. His wife turned to him and said, "See! You don't have to be ashamed of your failures because even through your failures you were teaching the next generation valuable lessons."

Through my father's failures I learned many great lessons that have helped me be a better man. I believe those lessons I learned can affect my sons and the next generation also, if I will not be ashamed of them and share them openly and honestly.

In fifty years of my life I have met some of the greatest men of our time. In these encounters I have always taken the opportunity to ask each man two questions.

1. What is the greatest thing you have ever done in your life?

2. What is the worst thing you have ever done in your life?

The dialogue has been quite interesting! I have heard many answers, some of which I have been astounded by and others, well, not too surprised. The stories that I have been told to go with some of the answers to these questions have been remarkable. Let me explain. I am not talking about answers that most people would want to hear, because they would not be juicy gossip, or earth-shaking, or even embarrassing stories, but for me, many of the answers were so thought-provoking that I still remember the heart behind each answer. I heard a famous man and author asked one day in an interview. "You quote so many great men in your speeches and books but I know you have never met the majority of them, like Abraham Lincoln, or Henry Ford." The man being interviewed responded with something like this. This is what I remember him answering and is not a direct quote. "I know that these great men who had died before I was ever born had much to impart in my life. But of course, how could I meet them? They were long gone from the earth by the time I was born, so I realized one day that if I wanted to know the man I needed to read his books. By reading books he wrote and words written about him, I could know the man."

A great communicator isn't one who is always talking, but many times is the one who listens.

I took that to heart and began to apply that principle to my life from that moment forward. I wasted no time and began to take any opportunity I was given to get to know these great men whose paths crossed my life path. Just remember to be courteous, and never impose yourself on another person. Always be polite and never be rude. When the proper opportunity arises, don't squander it. Always be respectful, even when you don't agree with their opinions. You asked the questions now be respectful of their answers. Never argue with another person's opinion when you have asked for it! These are times to learn from others whether you agree or not. It's not a time to debate, but learn to listen. Remember, you can always do what my wife says, "Eat the hay and spit out the sticks." She got that phrase from a beloved man who imparted great things in her life, Kenneth E. Hagin.

One day our sons had the opportunity to meet some professional athletes. When they approached them in the lobby of a hotel just to say hello, the men asked them, "Where are you going?" Harry III and Roman answered the men and then added, "Our dad always says, 'Don't impose yourself on other people's time. Be quick, be courteous, and be quiet.'" In other words, I always told them to not waste other people's time. Use your manners, listen, and learn.

The men were so impressed with our sons that they said to them, "Wait a minute! Do you have time to talk? Do you have a camera? Let's take some pictures together!" Harry and Roman said they did have a camera and they took pictures with many of the athletes and talked with them for a few minutes. When it was over, the men actually said, "Thank you," to our boys and followed up with more questions of their own.

They asked Harry III and Roman, "Who are you boys? What are you doing in this hotel?" This gave Harry and Roman the opportunity to share with the men that they were traveling with their parents and that they are ministers alongside us. They explained that we were upstairs in the hotel room preparing to minister in a service.

The men interrupted them and said, "That's why you are so polite. You know we are Christians too." They called over more athletes and said, "These young men are believers as well!" Harry and Roman met many of the men they had admired for their athletic abilities and because they were polite they found out that many were believers in Jesus Christ!

Now let's apply what we just learned to an even greater principle. When we want to know God as Father, then we need to realize that we may not be able to touch Him in the flesh.

> Read His book and you can know the Man!

We may not be able to sit down with Him across the kitchen table and interview Him. We may not be able to take long walks and have drawn out conversations in this natural realm, but YOU CAN READ HIS BOOK! When you read the book, you can know the man! Or in this case, when you read the Bible, you can know who your heavenly Father is! Once you learn who He is, then whether it is in the natural realm or not, you can take long walks and talk with Him. You can sit at the kitchen table and learn from Him. You can even seek Him with all your heart and even though you may not be able to touch Him, He will touch you! He will touch your heart and little by little begin to teach you His ways of doing and being. God is not a man, that's true. The Bible tells us in the book of Numbers (23:19) that God is not a man, and I think that is a good thing. There are plenty of men on the earth who we can learn from, and be friends with, and even glean fatherly wisdom from, but there is only one God who is Lord of all and King of kings, and He longs to be our Father.

II Corinthians 6:17-18

17*Wherefore come out from among them, and be ye separate, saith the Lord, and touch not the unclean thing; and I will receive you.*

18*And will be a Father unto you, and ye shall be my sons and daughters, saith the Lord Almighty."* (KJV)

God is a spirit and He is not a man that He should lie. God cannot tell a lie, it would be contrary to His very nature. God is truth, therefore He cannot lie to you or to me or to anyone else. So if you believe that God is truth, and that God is not a man, then you can also believe that His Word is true too. God, Almighty God, for some reason unknown and unexplainable to our human thinking, wants to be our Father. There is no doubt that we need Him. We need a father, not just a father, we need **the Father!**

I have so much for which to be thankful. My father chose to give me life. He and my mother chose to have a third child. Even though my life-learning experiences with my earthly father were not the typical father/son experiences that one usually remembers or even writes about, I would not be who I am today if not for those life-learning circumstances and situations.

Many times **we have to know where we came from before we can find out where we are going.** For that I am grateful. But it doesn't mean I have to accept those ways for my children. And it doesn't mean that I have to be bitter about them in my life either. I can simply learn from them and move on into my own God-given role as father and hopefully make choices that will be beneficial for our sons and their futures.

My heavenly Father destined me for life. My earthly father was the vessel God used to bring forth my life. My mother taught me about life. My wife taught me about love. Our sons showed me how to live life and our daughter makes me anxious for eternal life!

Since beginning to write this book, I was honored to be offered an honorary degree of Doctor of Divinity from Heritage Seminary and University. At first, I told Cheryl that I was going to say, "No thanks. That's not who I am. I'm just not that type of person." You see, I never got a college degree, so I didn't think it was proper to receive an honorary degree. It seemed like to me, if I were to accept it, I would be patting myself on the back, like I was proud or something of what I had done, etc. I didn't ever want to come across prideful, I guess. I was always of the mindset that 'someone else' deserved that type of honor. But as a friend said to Cheryl, "Finally, someone who worked for an honorary degree is getting one."

Well, Cheryl would not hear of my not accepting it so I asked a dear pastor friend of mine, Dave Williams, what he thought that I should do. He immediately said, "You need to accept this honor. Millions of degrees are earned but few honorary degrees are given." Then he went on to say something that sealed it for me, "You need to accept it for your sons, because it will let them know the value of what you have done on this earth, and the effect your life has had on people. You are being recognized for your life's work." So on May 21, 2010, I accepted an honorary Doctorate of Divinity degree from Heritage Seminary and University in Kissimmee, Florida. I was truly honored by it, but honestly I was even more blessed seeing my wife, Cheryl, throughout the ceremony as she was moved to tears over and over again. She said that she was crying because she knew what it had cost me to be honored in this way, the road that I had walked to get to this point. She said that she was so proud of me and thankful that others saw what she had always seen within me. She said, "I am so proud of what you have become as a man of God."

Then I received two text messages from our sons. From Harry III, "Congratulations, Doc!" luv u, and from Roman, "Proud of you, Pop!" luv u O.G. (O.G. stands for 'Old Guy,' his basketball nickname for me). Yes, I am blessed, not because of what I have done, but because of what my Father in heaven has done with me!

> We can make a choice to not repeat the failures of the past and not allow our past to predict our future.

The circumstances of life can cause us to turn out a certain way, but the good news is that by the choices we make, we can be different! We can move forward and never look back, repeating who we used to be over and over. Remember, one definition of insanity is doing the same thing over and over and expecting a different result. We can change. We can be different. We can accept where we have come from and forgive what needs to be forgiven, including our own mistakes at times. And we can make a choice to not repeat the failures of the past and not allow our past to predict our future. We can learn to be better, not bitter. We can learn to be happy, not hurt. We can learn to accept the things we cannot change and try our very best not to repeat them.

If not for my heavenly Father teaching me how to be an eternal son, I would still be lost, without hope of a future. But I have made the right choice. I have accepted Jesus Christ as my Lord and Savior and I have been adopted into the family of God. Now, without hesitation I can say, if not for my Father, I would not have an eternal future. But I do – with my Father who let me start in His thought life, sent me to this earth through the womb of my mother, and the seed of my father, to live, learn, and choose Him forever. Now I have a guarantee on where I am going.

What's better than knowing where you have come from?

Knowing where you are going is better! I am heaven-focused, and eternally-destined, as God

Longing for a Father

Almighty is my Father. The longing in my heart now is less and less for this earth and more and more for Him.

Father, I long for You!

> If not for my heavenly Father teaching me how to be an eternal son, I would still be lost, without hope of a future.

Chapter Sixteen

The L's of Fathering

Psalm 68:4-5 in the Message Bible says, *"Enjoy God, cheer when you see him! Father of orphans, champion of widows, is God in his holy house."*

Isaiah 3:4 in the Amplified Bible reads, *"And I will make boys their princes, and with childishness shall they rule over them [with outrage instead of justice].*

I Corinthians 4:14-15 (AMP), *"I do not write this to shame you, but to warn and counsel you as my beloved children. After all, though you should have ten thousand teachers (guides to direct you) in Christ, yet you do not have many fathers. For I became your father in Christ Jesus through the glad tidings (the Gospel).*

What are the L's of Fathering?

Limits

Leaders

Love

Laughter

Lord

Longing for a Father

Limits
Leaders
Love
Laughter
Lord

We were in a service recently, listening to a wonderful pastor from Michigan giving a message and an explanation on why we have what we have in our society today. He explained in detail what he saw as the biggest problem in our country, NO FATHERS! He talked about what we have when we have no limits, no leaders, then no Lord!

As I listened, the Lord began to give me this chapter on what we should be doing to try and undo what has not been done! As I meditated on what this pastor was saying, the Lord began to give me even more L's to complete the whole picture needed within our society to undo a fatherless generation.

II Corinthians 6:17-18 (AMP) states, *"So, come out from among [unbelievers], and separate (sever) yourselves from them, says the Lord, and touch not [any] unclean thing; then I will receive you kindly and treat you with favor. And I will be a Father to you, and you shall be My sons and daughters, says the Lord Almighty."*

God has given us a promise that He will step in and be what we did not have in our own fathers. He promises us that when there has been a gap in our lives from a lack of fathering that He, God Almighty, will fill the earthly gap with His eternal fathering presence! But we must accept Him as father. We must let Him be who He says He is in our own personal and daily lives.

Let's take this from the opposite position, one in which it is so easy to see, as we are living in that exact portrait in our society today. When there are no fathers we have:

NO LIMITS

NO LEADERS

NO LOVE

NO LAUGHTER

NO LORD

When we have **NO LIMITS** we will have a godless and lawless society. We, as fathers, must put limits on our children, for if we don't then who will? We have generations of limitless kids who have no discipline, or guidelines to live their lives by, because they have no fathers. There are biological fathers, yes, sperm donors, but where are the fathers that are respected and can, by their own example, lead the children? No, not many of those kinds of fathers are still living and breathing in our world. Fathers, rise up!

There are very few fathers even in the home anymore, and most of them who are still actually physically in the home are not 'fathering' God's way. There is no one at home to be the father's example. We have many teachers but few fathers the scripture said. That was written thousands of years ago, but it could have been written today, as this is where we are in history... many teachers, but few fathers. (I Corinthians 4:15, AMP)

I hear so many adult parents (I call them 'parents' loosely) say to their children, whether in actual words or in their lack of action, "Go to school and get a teacher to show you; get a coach to help you; it's their job." Whether these words are ever spoken or not, that's what the children hear. These good people are a blessing, as we believe teaching is a calling from God, but these are not who should be doing the majority of the teaching, imparting into or even rearing of our children! But so many kids hear from their parents, "You're on your own. I'm busy. Figure it out. Learn it on the street." And the latter is what most of our boys and even some of our girls have done. They have learned life lessons out there on the dangerous and lonely streets of life.

> The more time you want to spend with your children when they are young, the more time they will want to spend with you when you are old!

You might be saying, "I never said those words!" And you probably didn't, but it's not so much what you *are* saying but maybe what you *are not* saying! It's not what you *are* doing, as much as what you *are not* doing! Children hear as much in our body language and actions as they actually hear our words. They hear us say, "That's why teachers get paid to teach you. That's why coaches coach, so they can give you what you need. That's why you learned to read so you can gain knowledge from a book. That's the way I learned life – on the street and I turned out pretty good."

Well think again, and take a good long look in the mirror! Maybe you didn't turn out so good when you take an honest look at yourself! Maybe a few more limits would have helped you be a better parent, father, and mother today! It's not too late!

Remember, fathering is like making an investment and getting a return. The more time you want to spend with your children when they are young, the more time they will want to spend with you when you are old! Children are not an expense, but an investment. If you think of them as an expense, then they will be that in your life.

Proverbs 23:7 (AMP) states, *"For as he thinks in his heart, so is he. As one who reckons, he says to you, eat and drink, yet his heart is not with you [but is grudging the cost]."*

If you think your children are an expense they will be just what you think of them. If you think they are an investment they will be just what you think they are! Investments always yield a return in the long run; don't give up. The harvest of your much planted seeds will return to you multiplied.

I remember one Christmas when the children were small, we wanted to show them the importance of making an investment in others. Cheryl and I talked to them and explained that some children didn't have families, homes or toys to play with, and that these children needed help. Harry III, Roman and Gabrielle began to understand and it was not long before they excitedly began to ask what they could do to help. We suggested that they take a toy from their own room, a toy that they valued, and donate it to a child who would enjoy that object and love it as they had. We were so pleased and proud of our children as they searched for a toy to present as a gift for a child that they would never even meet.

The lesson in giving did not stop there. Later, I took the children to Wal-Mart, so they could purchase a gift for a child in need, as well. The children selected their gifts and paid for them with their own money. So, back to the car we went, each child swinging their Wal-Mart bags, happily chatting about the events of the day. Once we were inside the car, I turned to each of the children and asked them for their receipt. Harry handed his over and I noted his very generous gift selection that had totaled $20.00. I told him that Mom and I were very proud of him and then handed him a twenty dollar bill, and then another twenty, explaining that he had reaped a tremendous harvest on his investment. Next, Gabrielle presented her receipt. She had selected a gift of $10.00. I told her she had done a beautiful job and that her generous and unselfish actions had made her mama and daddy, and Jesus, so very proud of her. I handed her a ten dollar bill, and then another ten. Her beautiful blue eyes shone as she received the return on her investment. Then came Roman's turn. What do you think my youngest son said to me in that moment? "Daddy! Can I go back in?" Trying not to laugh, I asked him for his receipt. His gift selection had topped out at around $2.00. So, I handed him two dollars, and another two dollars, and the point of being a generous, joyful giver was illustrated by our three children.

Proverbs 22:6 (AMP) says, *"Train up a child in the way he should go [and in keeping with his individual gift or bent], and when he is old he will not depart from it."*

And when he is old... how I wish the Bible would have said when he is 22 years old, or 18 years old, or 35 years old! It did not say when a child will be 'old' or mature. But it does say that when they finally get to that mature stage, they will not depart from their training. What a promise!

Being a father is not a 'when I feel like it' job. You conceived them; you helped them get to this earth, now help them finish their race and spend eternity in heaven! Help them live forever! It's your job, God trusts you to do it, so do it!

Knowledge, boundaries, responsibility, and consequences of choices and actions cannot be taught from a book. They must be learned from fathers to children in a daily, ongoing relationship basis. Greater knowledge is seen more than read. Whether children know it or not, they want limits. They want to know where the lines of right and wrong are for them in their daily lives.

Children are always going to be just that, *children.* It's up to us as parents to train them to 'not touch the stove,' 'don't follow the crowd,' 'who you hang with is who you will become,' 'what you linger with lingers on you,' etc. Most children act like they don't want rules but in reality it is the limits in their lives that teach them what to avoid. If they have no limits they will never learn what to stay away from. If the limits are not clear, then the gray areas become the norm in their lives. A little lie becomes acceptable. A little less truth becomes the norm in their conversation. A little sin isn't so bad. They will think that their definition of a 'good person' will get them into heaven. Unless you give them the truth, they will never know the truth!

> Fathers, lead your children! Good leaders produce leaders!

If you were not fathered God's way, that does not mean that you can settle for not being a good father yourself. With each new generation comes new responsibility and a new opportunity to change the next generation for the greater good of all mankind. God did not put 'pretty good' or 'I've settled for what I have now' in you. He put *greatness* within you and that same greatness is in your children. It's up to you to see it, and pull it out!

The fast track to empowerment in one's life is through mentoring, through fathering!

When there are no fathers there are **NO LEADERS**. Kids today want someone to show them the way and how to do it. They gravitate to someone who has done it before, and they want their experiences in life to influence their decisions. Even gangs have leaders and they are becoming quite effective in our society today. If we, as fathers, would take our leadership positions, children would not look elsewhere for leadership in their lives. Leadership is not dictatorship. A dictator makes slaves. A leader makes more leaders! Leaders produce successors, and successors exceed their leaders.

My wife says it best, "YOU MANIFEST WHAT YOU ARE FULL OF." What have you manifested, what have you produced, what are you producing? You might think it's too late to do anything about it. Having come from a father who was a car dealer, every year they shut down and retooled for the next model year. Why would they stop production? So they could tweak the production line and in some instances completely change the model, then they would start back up with a newer, better model. Some of us need a complete retooling but actually I believe we all just need a little tweaking. And you know what, it's never too late. Take this to heart, **it's not how you start the game, but how you**

finish. Let's all finish well. But to finish you must start... so let's get going.

Sports teams have leaders, businesses have leaders. In every successful walk of life you will find structure with strong leadership at the top. God's kind of strong, godly family starts with strong leadership from the father. In some cases, single mothers have to set the example, but more by pointing the way to God as the ultimate Father than by trying to be fathers themselves. Mothers have a more than full-time position to fulfill on their own. Single moms cannot be both the father and the mother! God has given single moms hope and help through the scripture we began this chapter with, in Psalm 68. He promises that HE will be the father to the fatherless. That's a promise you can take to the bank of life. That check will always cash!

Why does an NBA coach make multiple millions of dollars a year? Because the team needs and wants a strong leader. Warren Buffett was recently paid over $2,500,000.00 just to have lunch with someone. Why? Because the person who paid that huge amount wanted an impartation, a mentoring session, a type of fathering empowerment from Mr. Buffett. Even politicians have interns who work virtually for nothing so they can be around the leadership to learn and grow. They want to receive an impartation from the one they are submitting to during that portion of their life. Gangs bring in the leaders to give their testimonies to effectively recruit new members. We lead not by what we say as much as by what we have done, and by what we do. We lead by example.

The church should be the greatest example of leaders in the world. Cheryl recently went to Texas to preach in a ladies conference. A friend of hers was preaching first, then Cheryl followed. Her friend said that the church should be the best walking, talking infomercial for God that there is! Whether we like it or not, we are an infomercial. But the real question is what are we selling? What are we proclaiming? What are we imparting to those who are watching and listening?

We must be careful that the people who are in the church do not become more filled with sinful ways than the world we live within! In I Corinthians 5, Paul is addressing a particular act of sin that was going on within the confines of the church. Men were sleeping with their father's wife! It was probably a step-mother, but regardless whether it was incest or a step-mother situation it was going on within the church. Paul was so sickened by the action that he wrote a chapter dealing with it. The offense violated even the social decency of the pagan world surrounding the church, and was a clear indication that the Corinthians had either a false notion about God's grace, or a too casual attitude about sexual immorality and sin!

Not only did Paul deal with the act, the sin itself, but the attitude of pride, and their general lack of repentance at the time of being found out.

I Corinthians 5:1-8 reads, *"It is actually reported that there is sexual immorality among you, and such sexual immorality as is not even named among the Gentiles-that a man has his father's wife! And you are puffed up, and have not rather mourned, that he who has done this deed might be taken away from among you. For I indeed, as absent in body but present in spirit, have already judged (as though I were present) him who has so done this deed. In the name of our Lord Jesus Christ, when you are gathered together, along with my spirit, with the power of our Lord Jesus Christ, deliver such a one to Satan for the destruction of the flesh, that his spirit may be saved in the day of the Lord Jesus. Your glorying is not good. Do you not know that a little leaven leavens the whole lump? Therefore purge out the old leaven, that you may be a new lump, since you truly are unleavened. For indeed Christ, our Passover, was sacrificed for us. Therefore let us keep the feast, not with old leaven, nor with the leaven of malice and wickedness, but with the unleavened bread of sincerity and truth."*

That word *sincerity* means literally *judged by sunlight,* in Greek translation. If we are to be the leaders God has ordained us to be, we must learn to judge our own lives, individually in the light of His presence and get on our faces and actually repent for our past actions or our lack of action. We must rise up and be the men of God, the fathers, He has called us to be. If not you, then who?

We who are in the church and representing our Lord and Savior need to lead by our lifestyle. We must purge our lives and our mouths from little white lies. When the phone rings and you don't want to talk to the person who is calling and you say to your child discreetly, "Tell them Daddy is not here," what message does that send to your child? It tells them it's okay to tell a lie if it benefits me. It's okay to tell a lie if I am about to be inconvenienced. Wrong! Don't teach them that lying is acceptable behavior before God!

When they hear you say that you need to do such and such today and you say, "I'll call in sick today. They owe me a day off anyway." Are you sick? Well, they know that! When the clerk at a store or the drive through window gives you too much change back and your response is, "Well, they are a big company. They won't ever miss it. Besides, this is God blessing me!" Oh, come on! God does not bless you through dishonesty! EVER! Be honest, live fruitful lives before those eyes who are watching you. Be a leader! Step up to the plate and start swinging!

Here are several qualities of leaders that you can check against the list of your own life.

1. Leaders know what they want. (Mark 11:24 AMP) *"For this reason I am telling you, whatever you ask for in prayer, believe (trust and be confident) that it is granted to you, and you will [get it]."*

2. Leaders have faith that they can accomplish what they desire. (Philippians 4:13) *"I can do all things through Christ who strengthens me."*

3. Leaders are not afraid to speak to the mountain on the way to their destiny. (Mark 11:23 AMP) *"Truly I tell you, whoever says to this mountain, Be lifted up and thrown into the sea! and does not doubt at all in his heart but believes that what he says will take place, it will be done for him."*

4. Leaders are not afraid to ask, pray, and believe. (John 16:23-24) *"And in that day you will ask Me nothing. Most assuredly, I say to you, whatever you ask the Father in My name He will give you. Until now you have asked nothing in My name. Ask, and you will receive, that your joy may be full."*

5. Leaders are not afraid to receive, to walk in their destiny. (Ask and you will receive!) Receiving was the hardest one for me. To receive from someone else, even from God I needed to humble myself. I am finally learning how to receive, but it took laying all my pride on God's altar.

Lead without having to say a word. Lead by example with your lifestyle. I have heard Cheryl say this for years, "Witness for Christ all the time, and when you have to, use words."

Where there are no fathers there is **NO LOVE**. We covered the definition of *father* in an earlier chapter. *Strong leader of the house.* We also covered the definition of *love* means *the face of the father revealed.* We make up our own definition of love which usually involves sex. Love

> When we have no fathers, love is not defined early in one's life.

is seeing the Father God face to face. That's knowing love to the ultimate definition. Since the Bible says that, *"...God is love."* (I John 4:8), then how can we even consider knowing what love is without knowing God!? It's impossible to know love without knowing the author of love. God is love. Know God and you will know love.

We cannot impart to our sons and daughters the love of God without first having it ourselves in our own lives. We cannot impart the love of God without owning the love of God! If you want your children to know love for all eternity, if you want your children to see love and be loved for all eternity, then introduce them to the author of the book of love. If you don't know Him, you cannot properly introduce Him! Get to know Him personally and intimately yourself. He is longing to be your Father. He is longing to know you and fill you with His kind of ultimate cleansing and freeing love. He is your Father; He longs for you to be His child. So what will you choose today? Where do you stand with Him? It's always been and it always will be your choice. He has already chosen to love you. He has already made a way for you to love Him, but He loves us so much, He gives us the choice to come to Him or stay eternally disconnected.

Let's talk about **NO LAUGHTER**. The Bible says in Proverbs 15:13 (AMP), *"A glad heart makes a cheerful countenance..."*

Proverbs 17:22 (AMP), *"A happy heart is good medicine and a cheerful mind works healing..."*

Proverbs 15:15 (AMP), *"...but he who has a glad heart has a continual feast [regardless of circumstances]."*

Psalm 126:2 (AMP), *"Then were our mouths filled with laughter, and our tongues with singing. Then they said among the nations, The Lord has done great things for them."*

"Laughter is the best medicine," is a phrase I have heard all my life. I married a happy girl. She laughs much. When others ask her about being happy she simply says, "Happiness is a choice, and I choose to be happy." When I first met Cheryl she had a little book called, "Choose to be Happy," and she recorded a song and sang it regularly entitled, "Choose to be Happy."

Cut! I have a side story for you. When Harry III was a little boy, just about three and a half years old or so, he would sing Cheryl's song, only his rendition was, *"I used to be happy!"* It was so cute, and that's the way he heard it, I guess!

Back to the point about laughter... remember that when Cheryl and I married, I was a very different man, and we were so opposite in many ways. She always had a smile on her face and I seldom had one. Recently, we were having lunch with some friends of ours who reminded us of this story. They had met both of us prior to our meeting and marrying, and thought Cheryl was this wonderful, happy minister who had so much going for her and who everyone loved. Everyone she met wanted to be around her because of her charismatic personality. The husband said when he first met me and tried to talk with me I didn't say two words and never cracked a smile. He thought, "What's with this guy?" Later they heard that we got married and he said, "She married THAT GUY?!" We all got a huge kick out of it. I laughed so hard and I still laugh thinking about it and how he said it with such emphasis on, "that guy," like did she lose her mind, or was she in a coma? "That guy?" She must have been in mental trauma! I tell you this because I want you to know how far the Lord has brought me, and how He has changed me. I'm still the man He created, but He has been tweaking me over the years. Living with my wife, laughter and joy are contagious in our household, even after the trials and devastations that we have been through.

Longing for a Father

When we celebrated our 25th wedding anniversary our sons took us to dinner. While we were eating, Mom asked the boys about their memories of us over the past years of each of their lives. It took very little prompting to get them started telling stories. All of a sudden everyone was laughing at the table, and trying to get in their memory over the others! It went something like this...

"Remember when Dad fell off the roof putting up Christmas tree lights?!"

"Remember when Dad fell off the roof cleaning the gutters?!"

"Remember when Dad fell off the roof while he was trying to paint the trim?!"

"Remember when Dad fell off the roof and landed in the air conditioning system?!"

"Remember when Dad got shocked and blew himself backwards into the air conditioning unit when he tried to rewire the pool pump?!"

"Remember when Dad got lost while driving from blah, blah, blah (this one had many starting and ending points of destinations as this has happened more times than we have pages to write about!)."

"Remember when Dad fell asleep at the wheel and wrecked the motor home?!"

"Remember when Dad sliced his hand open while using a box cutter to cut a candle out of a vase for mom?!"

"Remember when Dad burned off his eyebrows while lighting the gas fireplace with the flue closed?!"

"Remember when Dad burned off his eyebrows and his mustache while trying to light the gas grill?!"

"Remember when Dad burned off his eyebrows, his mustache, and his hair when trying to light the gas heater at Granny's house?!"

"Remember when Dad knocked Mom's front tooth out on live national TV?!"

"Remember when Mom's front tooth broke off in a Power Bar while we were driving through the Grand Canyon, and Dad tried to glue it back in with superglue!"

"Remember when Dad used to cut our hair like little Dutch boys?!"

After a few minutes, I said, "Hey, wait a minute! All your stories are about the stupid and silly things your dad did!" But we were laughing so hard that they could hardly even hear me! As I sat back and listened, I realized a few things. First of all, I was laughing the loudest of all. Second of all, our sons, and my wife were not laughing at me, but *with* me!

We laughed until we finally had successfully embarrassed ourselves and we had to leave the restaurant! Laughing is fun. It really is! The best way to laugh is to be able to laugh at yourself! That way, the world can laugh with you, too!

When there is no laughter, there is no healing, no happiness, no joy, and no peace. I believe laughter can heal what all the counseling in the world cannot fix. God promises us in His Word, that laughter does good like medicine. It can heal what ails you. It can mend the broken places. It can restore what has been taken. It can fill a home with happiness.

The last one I want to mention is the fact that we live in a society with **NO LORD**.

Matthew 6:21 is my favorite scripture. It is the motto for my life in so many ways. It is my mission statement in a nut shell. It reads, *"For where your treasure is, there your heart will be also."*

If someone has to say about another person, "Well, I think they are a Christian," I would say they probably are not. What gives them the idea or thought that you might not be a Christian? Does your life lived in front of others not have enough evidence to prove that you belong to Christ? Do people judge your actions, the fruit of your life and not see any evidence of Christ? What *do* they see? Do they say things like, "Well, they might be Christians but they miss church a lot. I'm not sure if they even go to church. I see them mowing their lawn on Sunday mornings." Or when they talk to you do they only hear you talk about the 'things' you want in your life? Or when you are in casual conversation do they pick up the underlying negative feelings you have about your mate or your boss? Do they hear words of judgment or words of grace coming out of your mouth?

Jesus said in Matthew 12:34 that, *"...Out of the abundance of the heart, the mouth speaks."* Jesus told the disciples in Matthew 15:11, that it is, *"Not what goes into the mouth defiles a man; but what comes out of the mouth, this defiles a man."*

I was on a plane a few weeks ago and Cheryl and I were separated in our seats. The man I was talking to was asking me all kinds of questions. He saw Cheryl get up and go to the bathroom and he asked me, "Is that your wife?" I answered him, "Yes." He went on to say, "She looks like she could be your daughter!"

As a side note, I'm married to a former Miss America; some call her a beauty queen. Well, your wife might not have the title "Miss America" but she is your beauty queen because you were smitten by her beauty and desired to spend the rest of your life with her and did not want anyone else to be with her, ever. The most beautiful woman you have ever laid your eyes on was and still is your wife – let her know that once in a while.

Back to my airplane story... the flight attendant came back up the aisle and said to me, "You have a great wife." The man beside me jumped in and said that he had no doubt that I did, and that she should hear about our sons. He went on to say, "They are a great family." In fifteen minutes beside this man on a plane, he knew about my love, about what I value in life, about the treasures in my heart, all because of our short conversation. What do people know about you after a few minutes of conversation?

God desired a family so He created humanity in His own image. Like a true parent, the Father that He is, He wanted us to be like Him, so He made us in His own image. When we messed it up as a human race, He made a way for us to be reunited with Him, through the sacrifice of His only Son, Jesus Christ. We deserve to go to hell, but Jesus went for us. He came from heaven, so we can choose to spend the rest of eternity with Him in heaven! What an amazing deal for us! We deserve hell, so Jesus went in our place. We don't deserve heaven, but we get to go anyway if we will only accept Him as who He is! He is my Lord! Is He yours? He longs to be Lord of your life!

God gave us His Word to help us establish correct limits for our lives. He gave us His Son because He knew we could not live by the rules and that we would need a Lord to help us.

Leaders read and readers lead!

I want to end this chapter with one more thing. I heard Pastor Dave Williams recently teaching. He was teaching on leadership and listed 8 traits of a spiritual son.

A spiritual son...

1. Inspires trust in his leader
2. Encourages his leader
3. Is accountable to his leader
4. Is like-minded in his soul with his leader
5. Sincerely cares about similar things
6. Does not seek his own agenda

7. Has proven his character over time
8. Is someone who serves alongside his leader

I wanted to share them with you. Examine your own life and see if you are a true son. If you are, then you can honestly say you are living life with...

LIMITS

LEADERS

LOVE

LAUGHTER

AND ABOVE ALL, HE IS LORD!

Chapter Seventeen

It's Okay to Say You're Sorry

It's called forgiveness. Many times we think of saying that we are sorry, but then we decide not to because we have been told that it is a form of weakness for men. What a lie to keep us all bound up in pride! It's not weak to say you're sorry. In fact, it may take the greatest strength of all, humility. When Jesus was on the cross and had an opportunity to come off the cross because He was after all, Jesus Christ, the miracle-working Son of God, He was living in a flesh body but He was also God incarnate.

Before He ever got to the cross He was so tempted to back out on His assignment that angels had to minister to Him. As the Bible describes, He sweated drops of blood through His pores. He was under tremendous stress in His physical body, His mind, and His soul. We know He wanted to change His destiny by the profound words He spoke in His prayer (Mark 14:36), *"And He said, 'Abba, Father, all things are possible for You. Take this cup away from me; nevertheless, not what I will, but what You will.'"*

Such a simple, yet profound statement of submission. That statement from Jesus' lips tells us that His will was to not go to the cross, as He stated that He would not fulfill what He wanted, but He submitted to the ultimate will of the Father.

> Forgiveness is a willful act on our part to turn a person loose.

The Bible tells us in the book of Isaiah that Jesus was then beaten beyond recognition. He was nailed to a cross and hung between two thieves. And even on the cross, one of the thieves hanging next to Him tempted Jesus by asking Him to be who He said He was. He said in Luke 23:39, *"...If You are the Christ, save Yourself and us."* Jesus did not give in to the temptation but went ahead toward redemption for us through His suffering. In Luke 23:34, He stated the most life-changing statement of all when He said, *"...Father, forgive them, for they do not know what they do."*

Forgiveness. It's not for the one who deserves it, most of the time. Forgiveness is a willful act on our part to turn a person loose. Freedom for the one who does not deserve it, that's what real forgiveness is. It's a choice for the forgiver, not the forgiven. It's an act, especially in the beginning. It's an action of the mind, and will, and soul and spirit.

One definition of *forgiveness* is [2]*to pardon an offense, and to give up resentment against or the desire to punish or pardon the offender.*

I mentioned before that my wife says this many times, "Unforgiveness is like drinking poison and expecting the other person to die."

Saying you're sorry is actually putting you in the position to be forgiven. Admitting that you were wrong and wanting to come clean and say you are sorry puts you in the right place to at least ask for forgiveness from the one you may have hurt or offended. Whether you purposefully did something wrong, whether you unknowingly hurt someone, or whether you are fairly certain you didn't do anything wrong but you still want the relationship to be restored, saying you're sorry is a great action of courage and strength.

A coward ignores; a courageous person steps up to the plate and says they are sorry and asks for forgiveness. Cheryl says that having to be right isn't always worth it. She says that many times it costs you more in your relationship to have to prove your 'rightness' than you would like to pay in the long run. Sometimes just being quiet takes much more strength than defending yourself when you feel you are being 'done wrong.' A wise person picks their battles, and usually only engages in the ones worth fighting and absolutely only in those you can win!

Winning is not about proving yourself worthy, or being right. Winning is when a relationship is strengthened and when truth prevails. We win when others get ahead and we learn to put ourselves aside. Take a little time and read Jesus' example of unselfishness in Philippians 2 from *The Message Bible*. It's hardly ever worth it to disagree. Many times, by simply saying in your mind that you 'agree to disagree,' you can win the victory of peace more quickly.

I am not saying to be passive, or to not engage. I am saying there are battles worth fighting, but when it comes to those we love, there should never be two sides. If there are, then that means we are on opposite positions. How can a house divided against itself stand? The Bible says it can't! (Mark 3:25)

In Matthew 18:19-20, *"Again, I say to you that if two of you agree on earth concerning anything that they ask, it will be done for them by My Father in Heaven. For where two or three are gathered together in My name, I am there in the midst of them."*

> "Don't be sorry; be different."

Agreement brings Christ on the scene in our lives, marriages, families, homes, well everywhere we agree, He promises He is there! So the opposite of that statement must be true as well. When we disagree He is not there among us!

Above all else, we need King and Lord Jesus to be with us. So whatever it takes to learn to live at peace and in agreement, find a way to do it! Try to find a common ground and move forward from there. You might be the one that is right in a certain situation or you might think you are right, either way you could still cause a breach. The Bible says that if someone has something against you then YOU GO TO THEM! (Matthew 5:23-25) You start the process of reconciliation. That is the act of forgiveness and the beginning of the forgiveness process.

I used to hear Cheryl say to the children, "Don't be sorry; be different." I think that came out of the fact that as children they learned that if they would repent quickly their sins would be forgiven quickly! But after a period of time, Cheryl as Mama, learned that many times they were simply saying the words, "I'm sorry," but there was no corresponding action to those words. She began to say to them that sorry was not good enough. She was trying to teach them a different way of *being.*

Being different means I am going to make a change in the way I respond to a particular situation or event. By changing my actions and my attitude, many times it helps me not to be a 'repeat offender.' The word [3]*repent* in the ancient Hebrew language has a unique definition. It means *to burn the house.* What? Where in the world did that definition come from? Well, the ancient Hebrew was written more in the lines of stories than actual phrases and words. Usually every word had a story that went with it. In the case of the word *repent*, the corresponding story went like this.

When an enemy nation would come in and take captive a city, a group of people, etc. they would march them away from their homes. Once a safe distance away, they would then have all the people who were taken captive look back to where they once called home, and as they burned the entire village to the ground they were made to watch. Why? This was to prevent them from daydreaming of returning to where they came from! This gave them nowhere to long to go back to, nothing behind them.

In our lives, repenting should mean that we actually believe what the Bible says that we are separated

Repentance should bring a corresponding action of actual life change!

from our sins once we are forgiven! Repentance should bring a corresponding action of actual life change with it.

I don't believe that it is possible to go back and repair the past. The scripture is plain in Isaiah 43:18-19, which says, *"Do not remember the former things, Nor consider the things of old. Behold, I will do a new thing..."*

God does not even go back and change our pasts; He simply tells us to look ahead and move on to the new thing. If God does not bother to try and fix our pasts, we should not waste another minute worrying, or fretting over what is behind us. We can repent and ask the Lord to forgive us. We can ask others we may have hurt to forgive us. We can show a corresponding action of a changed heart and mind, followed by changed life and actions, and go on. Don't look back.

If you don't deal with your past though, it will most likely try to predict your future. Asking for forgiveness helps you turn loose and run to the future. It helps you untie yourself from haunting lying deceptions of the enemy of your mind.

When it comes to relationships within the family, husbands and wives, fathers and sons, fathers and daughters, mothers and sons, and mothers and daughters, we need to make an attempt to correct our past actions by not repeating them in the future. We need to find enough courage to talk it out with all parties involved, being as open and transparent, as humble and contrite as possible. People need to see your heart; the only way they can is by seeing your actions, your attitude and by listening to your words.

I can hardly believe it when people tell me all across this country that they do not have a relationship with their sons, or their daughters, or their fathers or their mothers. I want to grab them and tell them what I would give just to have another opportunity to have a relationship with my dad or my daughter. These separated and broken relationships are some of my greatest regrets in life; but they are not fixable from this standpoint so I wait. I wait for the repairer of the breach, the restorer of the streets to dwell in to come and take me home to be reunited eternally. (Isaiah 58:12)

When I see fathers and sons not speaking, I get so upset with them. Many will actually come to me and say, 'They did this to me," or 'They did that to me." Some will say, "They stole this from me," or

"They disrespected me, blah, blah, blah...." That's about all I hear anymore when people start telling me these types of stories. All I really hear is pride, pride, pride... all about me, all about me, all about me. I want to say to them, "You have no idea what you have in your life, in your hand, right in front of you! You should have it so bad! You should actually have a problem!"

Cheryl never counsels people because she says it's simple for most folks. They just need to "admit it, and quit it." She tells people to fast and pray for three days and if they still don't have an answer to their problem then she might talk with them. Of course most people don't want to seek God. Most people don't want to put their flesh under and have to stay at His feet until they get a breakthrough. Most people just want somebody to feel sorry for them, and tell them that they are blah, blah, blah... come on! Get over this and get on with your life! Jesus is coming! The Father is longing for you! You cannot long for Him, your Father, as long as every breath you take is all about you!

With my dad being in heaven for over forty years and our daughter being in heaven for over eleven years now, here's my best advice for you. If you have a loved one still with you here on this earth that you have a breach in your relationship with, go talk to them, and you do what you can to make it right. I'm not saying you were wrong, or they were wrong. It's not about right and wrong; it's about repairing the breach when possible.

I understand that forgiveness is a process and it's a building back of trust, just like building a rope bridge over a ravine. It's not done in a complete section at once. It's done board by board, foot by foot, and rope by rope. It takes time, energy, and effort. The boards which give you the ability to walk across the breach can only be any good when the ropes support it, and the ropes are anchored to each side of the breach. Think of you and your father, or your son, as each side of the ravine. You need to connect the breach. What do you start with? A rope; it's time to throw out a rope and see if it can be a rope that starts a bridge to a relationship. You might even find out it's a lifeline for yourself or someone else.

Using a visual of a lifeline with a life preserver attached to it is a good example of forgiveness. Without the float at the end of the rope it's not very good to keep you from drowning while you are in the water. But that isn't the end result really. It should sustain you while you are in the water. But ultimately, isn't the goal to get you back to the boat or shore, to solid ground for safety? And if you don't have a boat or a shoreline, what good is it to just float around in the water bobbing up and down, just waiting for the next wave to take you under?

A lifeline needs to be attached to something bigger than you. Forgiveness is bigger than you. In your own strength you can probably not forgive to the extent you need to be free. That's why Jesus was sent to forgive us of our sins for He is bigger and greater than we are. He has the ability by design to handle forgiveness. We, in our sin nature, cannot forgive as we should. Forgiveness is not a flesh act. It's supernatural; it's spiritual really and when Jesus Christ is our Lord, we can connect to the ability to forgive through Christ.

I John 4:4, *"...He who is in you is greater than he who is in the world."* It takes the greatness of who God is through Jesus Christ within us to walk out forgiveness, both receiving it and giving it. To forgive means we overcome our own flesh. Our flesh wants to protect itself, to isolate, and hide from pain, even the pain of healing!

Remember earlier I talked about the movie, "Home Alone" and the conversation toward the end of the movie between the old neighbor man and the little boy? At some point the little boy said something like, "Well at least you will know and you won't

> Fear can keep you separated from God and from those you love.

have to be afraid of what he will say anymore. At least you will know the answer."

Sometimes fear won't let us forgive or attempt to forgive. It can be fear of failure, fear of embarrassment, fear of rejection, or fear of the unknown. All these fears just keep you separated from those God has put within your life to love and accept you.

After we began our ministry together as a family, I had an opportunity to be reunited with family members that I had not seen in years and years. It all started with a dream that I had. Sometimes God talks to us through our dreams. I was in heaven I think, because my dad and I were talking. He was telling me that he was proud of me for the man I had become, for our children, my wife, our lives before God. At one point, he was talking about the many people who were in heaven because of our ministry. Then all of a sudden, he looked me right in the face and he said, "But where's my family?"

At that point, I awakened and knew in my heart what I had to do. The Lord orders our steps in ministry. We go where He sends us. We don't seek to go anywhere to preach. When a church or a pastor calls us to come, we take it to prayer and if we feel the Lord lead us to go there, then we go.

That's how we know that God orders our steps. Just a few months after my dream, I noticed that our ministry schedule had us booked in churches that were located in almost a circle around where I knew my family had last lived decades earlier.

I didn't try to get involved or help the Lord. We just went to the churches in that area when the time came to go. When we arrived at the first hotel, I told Cheryl that I thought we should try to make contact with my dad's family. Of course, I had no phone numbers, no contact information, but my assertive wife just picked up the phone book. She came right to a number and handed me the phone.

I didn't know what to do. I just couldn't call. What would I say? I had a dream! Hardly. Cheryl told me that it was not a problem and she started to dial the phone. I think I broke out in a sweat thinking about what they might say or not say... fear! It's irrational! Cheryl got an answering machine and she just loves those things! She says it's the best way to have a conversation, no one talks back and she gets to do all the talking!

She left this long drawn-out, southern message that would make anybody laugh listening to it! My mind began to race at what they would think when they heard this ridiculous message!

She started out with, "Hi! This is Cheryl Salem. I am married to Harry Salem, and we are in your area preaching tonight at ..." She went on and on as to where we were, what time the meeting would begin and that she would expect to see them soon. She ended it with how much she loved them, like only she could do!

There was no way on earth that I thought anyone would respond to such a message! We went to service that evening, and we started out like we normally do. Gabrielle sang first, followed by Roman worshiping, Harry III next, and then Cheryl sang. After Cheryl sang, I joined her on the platform and we began our time of ministry, preaching with two voices and one message. After each of the children sang, they left the platform, usually to go to the foyer, get a drink of water, go to the bathroom, and then back into the church so we could see them while we preach. Cheryl was singing when Harry III came running down the side aisle looking wide-eyed!

The children know not to interrupt a service unless it is very important, unless one of them needs our immediate attention. As Harry III approached the front, I went to meet him. Cheryl was still singing on the platform, but she could see the excitement in young Harry's face. Harry announced to me without hesitation, "Daddy, one of your relatives is here to see you!" I said, "Son, you don't know my relatives. I haven't even seen them myself in almost thirty years!"

Young Harry didn't miss a beat. He said, "But Daddy, they know me!" I looked up and before my very eyes, coming right down the middle aisle... it was as if I was reunited with my father after thirty years! All of my fears and uncertainties vanished as I rushed down the aisle. It took me back to the Sundays when all of our family would get together, to laugh, to play, to have fun. We opened our arms as we got closer, and melted into an embrace, reunited after thirty years. As I look back on that moment, all the memories of the past, or what was wrong, or what went wrong were gone, and we never had to deal with the past. We were just thankful for the present.

Cheryl just kept on singing. We found out later on, that the people in the church knew my family and knew we had been apart all those years. The tears flowed freely that night on all sides as all the differences, reasons, rights, excuses, and everything else melted away into the river of restoration.

Over the next few days, we had meals together, and I was able to see many family members that I hadn't seen in years. One started to say they were sorry, and I stopped them and said, "That's in the past. Let's go forward from here. I've forgotten it. You should too." And that was that.

One day, before we left their home, I knew I needed to talk to them in depth about their personal walk with the Lord. I knew they went to church. But I wanted to know where they would be spending eternity. I wanted to know if they would be spending eternity with me, and with my father. I tried to talk to them, but the little boy in me kept getting hung up on the right words to say. (Sometimes, the hardest people to witness to are your own family members.)

Finally, I took Cheryl aside and said, "You have to finish this." She said, "No problem." And promptly went inside the house to have a face to face with my family.

She sat them down at the kitchen table and recounted the story of the dream and why we were sent by the Lord to them. She asked them point blank where they were spending eternity. Like most people do, they hem-hawed around until she finally pinned them down. They finally answered that they hoped they were going to heaven. She confidently and boldly said, "Well, let's not hope so and miss heaven. Let's make sure." With that, she led them in the sinner's prayer, right there at the kitchen table.

Now my dad knows where his family will spend eternity. They will be right there in heaven with him!

In the following years, I have been so blessed to spend time with these precious members of my father's family. Some have graduated to heaven; some I get to see every year. I'm so thankful for God's restoration power.

With my own sons, I have had to learn to let them grow up. They are no longer little boys or even teenagers. My sons taught me more about forgiveness than anyone really. I was having a bad day one day and I got into a disagreement with one of my sons and we walked away upset. We still live in the same house and here is a good piece of advice. Don't have a discussion with someone standing up, because it increases the opportunity for someone to turn around and walk away. Always try to sit and talk it over, without standing up and walking out. Finish it, sitting down. I was being unreasonable to our son, and our other son was listening in on our conversation. Afterwards he came to me and said, "Dad, you are wrong." I didn't take that very well and replied, "What do you know about the situation?" He said that he knew enough to know that I was wrong. Whew, that was a tough pill to swallow. But I listened, unwillingly, at first. He was doing exactly what I had taught him to do... know what you believe and always, in every situation, stand up for your brother! Well, I was getting a huge piece of my own advice thrown right back at me!

Later my wife came to me and told me that I was wrong also. I told her that our other son had already told me so! I told her I didn't need all these people pointing out my flaws! You see, you have to be a really strong person to stand up to me, because I don't back down. I have had to learn to let my pride go, and admit when I need to be different. My wife reminded me that we had reared our sons to have strong opinions and to have strong convictions too. She told me that I had my point of view and they both had a different viewpoint.

When the children were younger and they needed reprimanding I remember that I used to get on their level to do so. I had to learn that I couldn't do it from a standing position. If you are 'talking down' to your children, I believe that's intimidation. I don't believe in talking down to our children, even though I have been wrong on more than one occasion in trying to intimidate them into doing the right thing! I have learned though, a decision based upon intimidation is not a heart decision at all, rather a fear-driven direction. It never sticks. Never correct to intimidate, but correct out of love, like our heavenly Father does. Our sons are taller and bigger than me, and I hope they remember this!

If you will kneel down and talk to your children face to face, the end result can be so beneficial. I remember one time in particular with Gabrielle, I knelt down and talked to her, explaining the situation and why there was a need for correction, and when I was done, she reached over and hugged me. Isn't that how it should end up... with a hug?

Of course, now our sons have grown much larger than me in stature, and even in the situation where I was wrong, and was told so, they were both much taller than their dad. I realized that they could have actually turned the tables on me and tried to intimidate me but they didn't. I realized that it took a lot of guts for them to stand up to me and then for our older son to come to me and say, "Dad, can I talk to you and not upset you? I believe you were wrong and too hard on my brother."

Thinking about it and knowing that I am no longer the smartest person in the room (which I know I never am, I was just trying to act like I was!) is refreshing with our sons. They are smart, and more importantly, they are wise beyond their years. We have trained them to think and make right decisions.

I went back and apologized and told our son I was sorry and I changed my decision as well. Now you might think I was relinquishing my authority to my son and that I was losing my position with him. No, I was cementing our relationship that said, whether right or wrong, we can communicate and we are both on solid ground together.

If you can never admit that you are wrong and everybody in the house knows you're wrong including you, what kind of a message are you teaching your children? That the leader has to be right, even when they are wrong? Teach your children to repent, by example. Be the first to repent and let them hear you say it. Let them hear you pray it! Let them hear you ask God to forgive you. Let them hear you ask your wife to forgive you. Let them hear you ask them to forgive you.

> Repentance is the strongest and most courageous position a man can take.

What have you taught then? That **repentance is the strongest and most courageous position** they can ever take. Forgiveness flows like oil when everything is warm. But when everything is cold, oil turns from a liquid to a solid.

It's hard to pour a solid! Keep things flowing freely in your relationships by warming up the environment.

Letting your children have an opinion and learning to listen to it, teaches them the importance of forming opinions, of thinking, and being wise. Communicating our feelings and letting our sons actually show their emotions and feelings has been extremely healthy in our home. It's important to them that I listen, and that I can humble myself before them, as well as before the Lord of my life.

Disagreements will come and go in life. If you think you can live without disagreements, you need to think again. That's a fairytale land. Resolving issues is harder, but has much greater rewards. Learning to say, "I'm sorry" isn't easy but the rewards are beyond imagination. Remember, "I'm sorry" begins with what 'I' am willing to do first.

John 3:16 states, *"For God so loved the world that He gave His only begotten Son, that whoever believes in Him should not perish but have everlasting life."* God gave His Son first, then He gave us the choice to choose or reject Him. It has to start with a willing vessel, a willing life. Remember Jesus said to the Father in the garden before His crucifixion, *"Not My will, but Yours be done."* Jesus put the Father God's desire ahead of His own.

So Jesus was a willing vessel to go through the pain and suffering of the cross for us. Anything we have to go through for forgiveness is just a little penance compared to what He suffered for us. But we must be willing to take the first step and be a willing vessel to have the reward of eternity and His ultimate forgiveness.

I want to close with this acronym for "FATHER."

F stands for faithful.

A stands for attentive.

T stands for trustworthy.

H stands for honorable.

E stands for enthusiastic.

R stands for righteous.

Be a faithful father, mother, son, or daughter in life. Be attentive to those who love you and whom you love. Be trustworthy in your relation-ships toward others. Mean what you say, and say what you mean. Doing what is right isn't always popular but doing what is popular isn't always right. Be honorable in every relationship in your life. Honor means to open the door. Without honor you will live a life of closed doors, closed hearts, and closed minds all around you. When you live honorably people won't say that they think you are a Christian. They will know you are by your life lived in front of them. They won't question whether they should allow their children to come to your home, but will say they want their children influenced by your life. Be a good influence on your children. If you don't influence them, someone else will. Be enthusiastic and encouraging to your children, and those you are in relationship with. Encourage them to be dream seekers and *you* be a dream seeker. Don't be a dream stealer in other's lives. Children want your approval. We all want approval. We ultimately want to hear, *"Well done, good and faithful servant."* Don't give your best to everybody in the world who doesn't really know you and give your leftover, no-energy life to those who care the most for you. And last of all, be righteous. Righteousness is not being perfect. There is no way we can be perfect. Only Jesus is perfect, but in Christ we can ever be in the process of being perfected through His grace and mercy. Righteousness is a free gift from God. We can't earn it. Don't try to pretend like you are perfect. Don't try to act like you never have had a fault! Be

> Doing what is right isn't always popular but doing what is popular isn't always right.

real. We can't be good enough. If we could have been, then Jesus would not have had to come and pay the price for us. So relax. You are not good enough, and you never will be on your own, or in your own strength, so take the pressure off of yourself and let Jesus be the Lord of your life. Because in Him, you move and have your being, and you are the righteousness of God, in Christ Jesus.

You are free, you are His Son, He loves you... He knows you are longing for a Father, and He is longing for you, too.

Roman, Dad and Harry III

Prayer of Salvation and Repentance

You know, every night I still like to hear our sons voices, whether it's via the phone, a text, or in person. I love hearing their voices. I never go to bed without telling them I love them and many times the conversation is short and sweet. Other times, we talk about the day's events or what's going on in their lives or ask and answer questions. But I love talking with them. Well, that is exactly how our heavenly Father is with us. Every day or night He would love to hear our voice, have a conversation, and even answer a few questions. I get that opportunity with my sons because we are in a good, right relationship. There is nothing wrong between us and we are in covenant. If you don't have that relationship with your sons, now is a good time to start, pick up the phone or e-mail them or even send a text, better yet get face to face with them, because there is something special in a personal touch.

Now when was the last time you had that type of conversation with your heavenly Father? Have you ever had a meaningful talk with Him, with actual questions and answers? You know, what amazes me most about God is that the same Creator who flung the stars from His fingertips and scooped out the oceans and formed the mountains has given us the opportunity to talk with Him! What's even more amazing is that He has the time to talk back to us!

Here's my question: Do you have that type of relationship with your heavenly Father or do you just have a Bible sitting on your coffee table? Maybe you have a necklace with a gold cross on it, or maybe you even go to church (on Christmas and Easter). One of my favorite stories in Acts 26:27-29 (AMP), when Paul is in prison for nothing he has done, and he is brought to King Agrippa and is told to plead his case, Agrippa finds no fault with him, but while Paul is talking, he is sharing his love of God and his Christian faith with him. And he makes a statement that says, *"King Agrippa, do you believe the prophets? [Do you give credence to God's messengers and their words?] I perceive and know that you do believe. Then Agrippa said to Paul. You think it a small task to make a Christian of me [just offhand to induce me with little ado and persuasion, at very short notice]. And Paul replied, Whether short or long, I would to God that not only you, but also all who are listening to me today, might become such as I am, except for these chains.*

One translation refers to the chains as bracelets, and in the King James translation it reads, *"Then*

Agrippa said unto Paul, Almost thou persuadest me to be a Christian." I want you to know that here Paul is in prison and in handcuffs, but that doesn't stop him from telling of his Father/son relationship with his heavenly Father. He sees his situation as an opportunity to lead the king, and everyone else who is listening, to the Lord. Yet the king said that today he was almost persuaded to be a Christian. In other words, he was saying, "Today I almost became a Christian and guaranteed myself of a Father/son relationship and a future with my Father in heaven for eternity." My question to you is this: Are you a Christian, do you have a relationship with your heavenly Father, and are you having a daily talk with Him? Are you going to heaven or not? It's black or white. Do you know that you know that you know if you closed your eyes here you would definitely open them up in heaven for eternity? Or are you almost a Christian? Almost isn't good enough. Going to church on Christmas and Easter isn't dwelling in my Father's house. Wearing a gold cross is only a symbol of what you want others to think of you, but it won't assure you a place at the Father's table. Having a Bible on display in your home will not guarantee you of that heavenly home with a mansion on the streets of gold for you for eternity. Almost isn't good enough. It's time to talk with your Father and I would love to be your mediator, your go-between, to introduce you to

Him and let you two take it from there. It's simple, just repeat these words. You don't have to repeat them from your mouth, but from your mind... your very being, from your heart to the ears of the Father.

"Lord, I ask You to come into my heart and forgive me of my past, my sins, my old nature, and make me a new person. I accept that Jesus Christ came from heaven, is the Son of God, walked this earth as a man, was crucified, died and buried, but rose on the third day, so that I could have everlasting life. Through His shed blood I have been forgiven of my sins and I live in the present with the guarantee of my future in heaven with Christ Jesus and my heavenly Father."

If you meant what you just said, you now have been introduced to your heavenly Father, go ahead have a talk with Him. Try it, you'll like it.

In Conclusion

The stories and events in this book are a recounting of my life and experiences over fifty years. To the best of my ability and memory, I have told them as accurately as possible. I have shared my life and my experiences with you, and hopefully these events that have marked my life will mark yours as well. This has worked for me and my future and I have found the peace of knowing that God is my Father. In knowing this, I believe I have become a better father as well. I am not saying this is an exact science by any means, because it all comes down to how each one of us individually believes and responds to that belief.

To those of you who read this book or any of our books, the views and opinions expressed are based on our personal lives and our interpretation of the Bible.

We pray you were blessed as you read these pages.

Endnotes

[1]"longing." Merriam-Webster Online Dictionary. 2009.

Merriam-Webster Online. 20 October 2009 *www.merriamwebster.com/dictionary/longing*

[2]"forgiveness." Def. *Webster's New World Dictionary*. 1995. Simon and Schuster Publishers, Pocketbook, Paperback edition.

[3]We have been very influenced by the work of Frank T. Seekins. See his *Hebrew Word Pictures* (Phoenix: Living Word Pictures, Inc., 1994).
www.livingwordpictures.com
Used with permission.

[4]Bettger, Frank, *How I Raised Myself from Failure to Success in Selling*. Prentice Hall Press, 1986.

It is important to note here that of this research, I only used that information which I found to be documented scientific fact. I am not endorsing these authors or any of their other writings found in these articles or any other articles in any way. As Brother Kenneth Hagin would say, "Eat the hay and spit out the sticks!"

About the Author

Harry Salem is a success story. He lost his father to leukemia when he was ten years old, but that adversity only caused him to narrow his focus and drive to succeed.

As a young man in his twenties, Harry quickly made a name for himself in the business world, becoming a successful business administrator. But he always knew that there was more; something was missing.

He met a beautiful girl named Cheryl, they got married and started their family, but it wasn't until the mid-nineties that Harry had an encounter with God that changed him forever. He let go of the pain of growing up without a father and of the stress of the mantle that had been placed on his shoulders at such a young age. He began to trust God, and he has never looked back.

Harry Salem is a minister of the Gospel. He and his wife Cheryl are the founders of Salem Family Ministries. They are parents to sons Harry III and Roman, and to daughter Gabrielle, who lives in heaven. Gabrielle passed away in 1999 at the age of six. This tragedy brought the family closer together, and the Lord began to use Harry and Cheryl to minister hope and restoration to other families in grief and mourning.

In the last few years, Harry has been hearing the voice of the Lord on the subject of fathering – God's way. His latest book, *The Rise of an Orphan Generation: Longing for a Father*, is geared to men and women who have not been fathered in God's way. Restoration can be found, and it is Harry's desire to bridge the gap between people's broken hearts of longing for a father, and to place them in the arms of the one true God who is Father of all. As Harry continues in ministry, God faithfully pours out His anointing and power through his life in a profound and mighty way.

Dr. and Mrs. Harry Salem II

Dr. Harry Salem

Salem Family Ministries
P.O. Box 701287
Tulsa, Oklahoma 74170
www.salemfamilyministries.org

*You can reach Harry & Cheryl at the above address.
Please include your prayer requests
and comments when you write.*

Other books by Harry and Cheryl Salem

For Men Only
Don't Kill Each Other! Let God Do It!
We Who Worship
Entering Rest – Be Still – A 40-Day Journey into the Presence of God
Obtaining Peace – A 40-Day Prayer Journal
2 Becoming 1
The Choice is Yours
Overcoming Fear – A 40-Day Prayer Journal
Every Body Needs Balance
From Grief to Glory
From Mourning to Morning
Distractions from Destiny
Speak the Word Over Your Family for Finances
Speak the Word Over Your Family for Healing
Speak the Word Over Your Family for Salvation
Covenant Conquerors
Warriors of the Word
*Fight in the Heavenlies**
*It's Too Soon to Give Up**
Being #1 at Being #2
A Royal Child
The Mommy Book
*How to Get a Balanced Body**
*Simple Facts; Salvation, Healing & the Holy Ghost**
*Health & Beauty Secrets**
*Choose to be Happy**
Abuse...Bruised but not Broken
You Are Somebody
A Bright Shining Place - The Story of a Miracle

**Call for availability*

The Salem Family

Be the strong leader in your home that your family, your children and your wife need and desire.

I would rather
fail at
something I
love, than
succeed at
something I
hate.

Where is your treasure? That's where you'll find your heart.

You may not
see yourself as
a man with
greatness, but
God has
already put
greatness
within you!

The Lord said,
“Your purpose
from this day
forth is to tell
My people...

"...if they would long for Me that much (as much as you long for your daughter), then I'll come quicker."